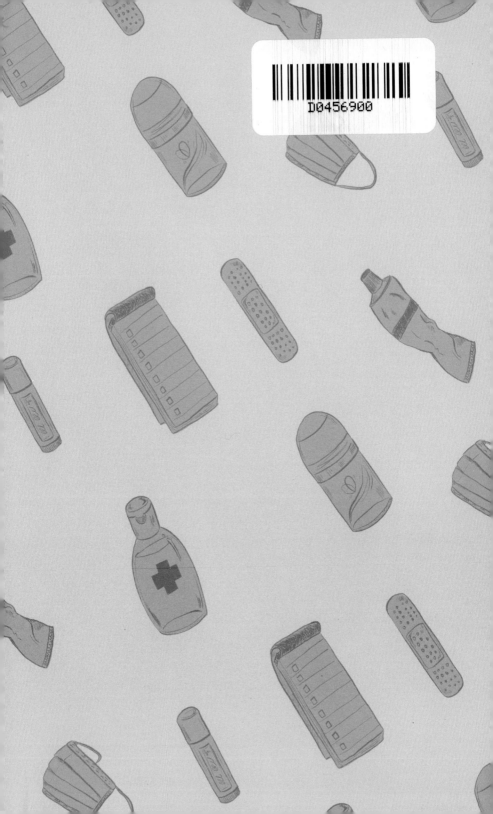

Anxious
Girls
do it
Better

Dedicated to Karen Banyai, for all her work raising this anxious girl, and Clementine, Beatrix and Peppa: may the good times be more plentiful than the bad as you voyage through life.

Anxious
Girls
do it
Better

A TRAVEL GUIDE FOR
(SLIGHTLY NERVOUS)
GIRLS ON THE GO

BUNNY BANYAI

ILLUSTRATED BY
ASTRED HICKS

Hardie Grant

EXPLORE

CONTENTS

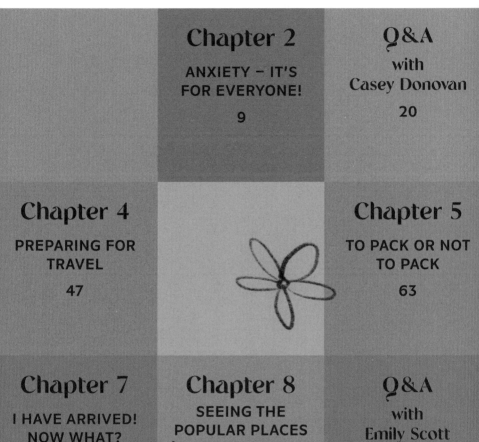

The Excess Baggage Of Anxiety

Does the thought of travelling or being away from home give you mild to moderate palpitations? You don't need to have an official diagnosis of anxiety or OCD to get something out of this book. This guide is intended to help you approach your next journey (big or small) feeling confident, prepared and, if not relaxed, at least comfortable enough to not require adult diapers and equine sedatives on the flight or road trip. It's filled with all the things I know about travelling with the invisible, excess baggage of anxiety. It also contains practical tips from a psychologist and a pilot, and anecdotes, tips and interviews from some exceptional women, all of whom have plenty of frequent flyer miles under their belts.

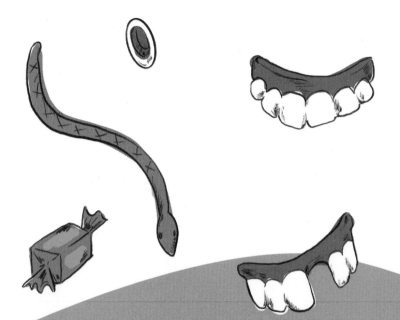

Who knows what combination of raw fish, hard liquor, soft cheese and cat faeces my mother treated herself to when she was pregnant with me, but whatever it was resulted in a singularly worried human being. I can't recall any time in my life where I might accurately have been described as *sangfroid*, or any of the other less pretentious words meaning 'chill'. As a newborn, I refused to nurse, probably because I was worried that my mother hadn't sanitised her breasts. As a child, I was scared of the dark, clowns, my bedroom, the back door, basements, *Doctor Who*, Grace Jones, the cover of one of my dad's Tom Waits records and the country. Though marginally less bonkers now, I am still a bulging pick'n'mix bag of fears and neuroses, which means that travelling triggers a few minor issues, like *the absolute certainty that I will die on a trolley in a foreign hospital while using Google Translate to try and say 'penicillin allergy' in Macedonian.*

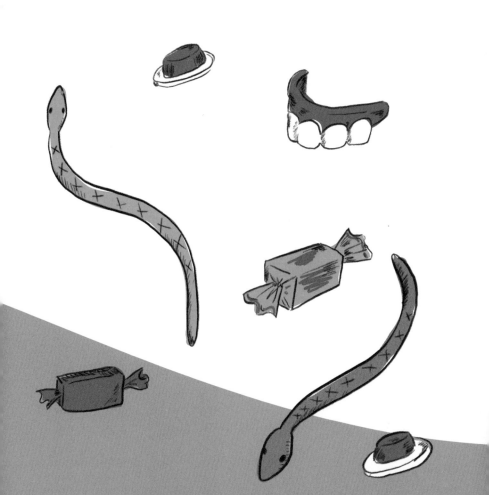

So, when I learned that writing this book would entail some solo travel, my reaction was one part glee, one part mewling kitten trapped in a drain. 'Well, who WOULDN'T want to go to New York and Kyoto!' I exclaimed, as my publisher politely averted her eyes from the extensive network of high-vis sweat patches breaking out across my body. 'I am very excited,' I said, 'and definitely not thinking about how I will asphyxiate alone in a hotel room due to a gas leak from a faulty air con unit!'

But despite ruining the armpits of a silk blouse and setting off every pacemaker within fifty yards, I knew I could not let my neuroses rob me of the opportunity to travel. Moreover, I could not face telling people that I turned down the chance to write a book about travelling with anxiety because I was too anxious to travel. Then, of course, COVID-19 entered the picture, black robes flowing, scythe in hand. The freedom to travel suddenly became a relic of the past, a Before COVID (BC) novelty.

At the time of writing, vaccines are being deployed across the globe at paces varying from impressively quick to maddeningly glacial, as we all pray that no new, vaccine-resistant variants rear their heads. As we begin to cautiously unfurl our tentacles into the wider world again, many of us will be doing so with considerably higher anxiety levels than BC.

After all, for much of 2020, and at least the early months of 2021, many of us were barely able to venture beyond our front doors, much less contemplate air travel. My hometown suffered a second wave of the virus that necessitated a months-long hard lockdown, 8pm curfew, and 5-kilometre radius in which to roam. As a consequence, just visiting my local supermarket now feels like scaling Everest. Sharing air with 400 strangers in a confined space for 17 hours will no doubt be quite a leap, indeed.

The spectre of the lingering pandemic – along with some of the stories contained within this book – might make it seem to you like travelling is a lousy idea, but the thing about travel is that even when it goes tits-up, it's wholly worthwhile. Every time you travel you learn something valuable: that you should never eat the capsicum dip in your inflight meal; that sneaking a cigarette in the smoker's booths at Abu Dhabi airport is equivalent to tossing your lungs into a bonfire; that an infected foot can't be ignored; and that sensible footwear is, sadly, a non-negotiable travel essential.

More importantly, travel broadens your view of humanity, revealing infinite variations on how to live a life. No matter how much terrible news comes out of it, the world is still filled with stuff to wow your mind and make you cry with joy and wonder.

There is nothing better than stepping out the front door of your hotel or apartment on the first day of a holiday, knowing that you have a whole city to discover and that within a week you will have new favourite cafes and falafel joints and parks and streets. That within a week, you'll have a whole lot of little routines specific to your temporary hometown. There are also rich rewards to be found within the borders of your own country, as plenty of us, locked out of or hesitant to venture overseas, have discovered these past few years.

The first time I visited Sydney, I was gobsmacked to learn that the place was lousy with ocean pools – big, beautiful pools carved right into the rock-shelves – and that not only did the local councils maintain them, but they were *free*. I live only a one-hour flight from Sydney, yet I spent a sizeable chunk of my adult life not knowing that the biggest draw was not the Harbour (which is a big deal, make no mistake) but the 35 ocean pools – surely one of the greatest gifts a city has ever bestowed on its citizens without asking anything in return. These are not lessons you can learn watching Netflix in bed, no matter how high the production values.

I took my first flight at age one and vomited all the way from Melbourne to Queensland. Since then, I have vomited on flights to Vienna, Budapest, Singapore, and in hotels in Palermo, Ortigia, the Swiss Alps, Fiji, Frankfurt, and Lyon. I loathe vomiting, so much so that in 2018 'loathing' turned to 'phobia', and I was diagnosed with emetophobia, or a fear of vomiting – another fun thing to add to my extensive medical records. Yet I don't automatically think about all the international toilets I've had my head in when I think about the places I've been. I think about the good stuff.

It is a pretty powerful testament to the positive effects of travelling if someone like me – who begins to fear winter at the beginning of summer and always sees the cloud before the silver-lining – has only rose-coloured memories of all the places she's been (except for Luton airport). You will never regret travelling, unless it involves drug smuggling or a botched nose job. The only event in which you should allow worry to trump over wanderlust is if a government advisory explicitly tells you to do so.

You may simply be slightly nervous at the idea of parting with your life savings in exchange for six weeks of the unknown. Or maybe the pandemic has shaken your confidence, which doesn't make you someone with an anxiety disorder but rather, a human being experiencing a normal reaction to a traumatic event. Besides, the prospect of travelling to somewhere new with only a wheelie bag for company could induce anxiety in a bar fridge.

But you should travel anyway. Read this book and pack your bags.

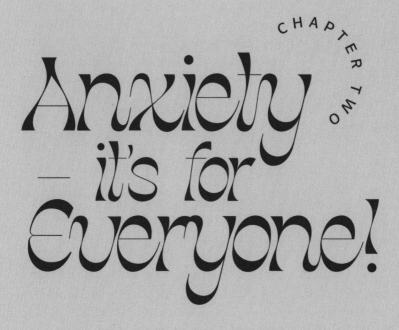

CHAPTER TWO

Anxiety — it's for Everyone!

Well-meaning friends and family can tell you anxiety is nothing to be ashamed of until they're blue in the face, but we often doubt the praise and reassurance of our loved ones. Nobody, for instance, has ever told me I look like Kate Winslet, except my own mother, which makes me question the validity of everything she's ever said to me, from cradle to adulthood. On the other hand, if, say, Adele were to tell you that anxiety is nothing to be ashamed of, you might pay a little more attention. It IS possible to be a VAP (Very Anxious Person) and a VIP (Very Important Person) and sell 120 million records.

Having anxiety does not preclude you from being a massive pop star, or the most famous talk show host of all time, or anything else, including a global traveller. Oprah, Chrissy Teigen, Amanda Seyfried, Liz Cambage, Emma Stone, Cardi B, Missy Elliot, Jennifer Lawrence and Sarah Silverman are all hugely successful. They have all reached the top of their game while grappling with anxiety. Fame, like herpes, is a great equaliser.

This is not to say anxious girls, or anyone else, should expect to sell 120 million records or score the lead in a Hollywood blockbuster because not all of us are destined for careers that soar from one vertiginous height to the next. One of the many misleading aspects of social media is the way it suggests, through filters, picturesque backdrops and straight-up bullshit, that everyone else is leading incredibly fortunate, creatively nourishing and unique lives. The reality is most people spend most of their lives dealing with the same mundane challenges of relationships, jobs, bills, housing and health. Nobody posts pictures to Instagram of paying an electricity bill at the local post office, renewing their car registration or wiping menstrual blood off the toilet seat, but this is – mostly – what life actually looks like.

Ideally, the moments of your life that aren't spent keeping a roof over your head and food in the fridge should be spent doing the things that make being a human, as opposed to a pangolin, quite a lot of fun – going to the cinema, watching a band, seeing live theatre and travelling. These are the unique gifts we automatically qualify for on account of being members of the human species.

I'm jealous of cats because they get to sleep for 18 hours a day, often on top of a hydronic heater. I'm jealous of birds because they can fly. I'm jealous of koalas because they sit in trees all day, and they don't need to be on welfare to support that habit. They are *applauded* for their adorable inertia. It's really not fair. But the thing is, that's *all* these animals can do. Cats sleep all day, but they don't do much of anything else. Birds fly, but not to biennales, or weddings, or to their favourite concert. Koalas do literally nothing but consume voluminous quantities of gum leaves all day. We humans can do so much *stuff* that's not available to other species, and this is the most compelling reason I can think of to not let anxiety call the shots. You do not want to miss out on all the fun human stuff. Recognise your anxiety, talk about it and get a management plan together from your medical professional.

The upside
of anxiety

Unlike its cousins, depression and bipolar, anxiety has never been sexed up for film and TV. There are plenty of films portraying beautiful mad girls losing their minds (usually with an ensorcelled suitor watching helplessly from the sidelines) while maintaining a voracious appetite for unhinged sex, but very few films have attempted to make anxiety a desirable trait. Worrying about germs on handrails and triple-checking the stove is off is not a turn-on. Of course, the reality of depression is distinctly unsexy too, but it's anxiety, we're led to believe from its on-screen depiction, that is the really *uncool* affliction. Betty Blue would never have worked if Betty was just inordinately scared of plane travel and flu season.

But I would argue that wanting to just *stay safe* and, you know, *alive* is not a massive turn-off. Ask not 'what has anxiety done *to* me?' but 'what can anxiety do *for* me?' A healthy awareness of life's dangers goes some way to avoiding preventable death and disease. I'm often grateful for my high levels of resting anxiety, which have at times tormented me, but have also frequently kept me out of harm's way.

When I was six, I was having a post-ballet class burger at McDonald's with my mother and brother and noticed flames and smoke coming from the kitchen, in full view of all the other diners. As I took in the spectre of the burning kitchen, I noticed a weird thing: no one else was reacting. Not one person. I couldn't believe it. So, I let out an almighty scream. No deer in the headlights denial phase for me before springing into action. Being permanently primed for the worst-case scenario, I had no problem recognising the worst-case scenario when I saw it. The other diners finally sprang into action and began to evacuate, moments before the fire brigade arrived. Now, I'm not saying I saved any lives that day, despite this being my preferred narrative, but my anxious, reactive nature at least ensured that we all hightailed it out of there that much sooner.

(On the other hand, the most relaxed boy I ever dated died in an avalanche in the Himalayas, which is not a fate that tends to befall anxious people. We understand that mountain climbing is frequently associated with 'negative patient outcomes', and we take sensible steps to avoid it.)

The other upside is that – stay with me here – anxious people are more fun to be around. We're more alert and we're more alarmed, which naturally makes us keen observers of life. The cool crowd in high school may be the nonchalant and effortlessly unruffled ones, but 90 per cent of the time those kids are relaxed and comfortable because *they are boring.* This is the great secret that no one tells you when you're a teenager. The cool kids are not anxious because *they don't think very much.* I wanted nothing more than to be one of the girls who slithered around the school yard, lazily tossing my awesome mane of flaxen hair behind my shoulders (cool girls, at least in the mid-90's always seemed to have extremely thick blonde hair – it was as if their healthy locks offered some kind of protective, pro-vitamin B insulation against the vagaries of high school politics).

Now, with the benefit of hindsight, I am very glad I wasn't popular. The girls I wanted to be like in high school went on to marry their high school jock boyfriends, hang out at places with names like Reef'n'Beef (Aussie surf'n'turf) and settle down in the suburbs, which is all just fine, but would have left me wanting. Neurotics are simply more fun to be around. They make music and art and movies and all your favourite shows on Netflix.

If you require any further proof, a 2015 study by genomic analysis company deCODE genetics revealed that visual artists, writers, actors, dancers and musicians in Iceland were 17 per cent more likely to carry genetic variants linked with mental health issues than the general population, and the number shot up to 25 per cent when the authors looked at a different data set from earlier studies conducted in the Netherlands and Sweden. Dr Kári Stefánsson, the author of the study, said, 'The results of this study should not come as a surprise, because to be creative, you have to think differently from the crowd.' So wear your anxiety with pride – you're in good company. And you might be the next Frida Kahlo.

Trust your instincts

Conventional wisdom does not generally apply when your temperament leans towards the worried. Ever since I was old enough to put my own pacifier back in my mouth, I've been counselled to follow my gut and listen to my instincts. But if I listened to my gut every time it rumbled anxiously, I would be mistaking a lot of serious digestive work (I eat plenty of legumes) for a signal from within telling me to stay at home with the blinds drawn for the rest of my life. When poet Mary Oliver asked the question 'What is it you plan to do with your one wild and precious life?', I do not believe 'spend most of it on the sofa watching Olympic figure-skating highlights' is the answer she had in mind.

In other words, if you are an anxious type, you must know that your instincts are not always reliable. On *innumerable* occasions, my instincts have told me that myself or a loved one is in mortal danger when, in fact, they were just stuck in traffic, listening to a podcast about Prince's best album (*Sign O' the Times*). Every time I know travel is on the horizon, I spend the hours between 11pm and 6am besieged by technicolour nightmares in which I'm the victim of a plane crash or terrorist attack. Clearly, my anxiety dreams are *not* prophetic. If they were, they would be about unpaid gas bills, debt collectors and excessively expensive dental work, not plane crashes and bombings.

This is not to say that instincts should never be followed, simply that you should always take a step back, whip out your forensic microscope and examine whether this is a fear based on reality or anxiety. That could mean talking to a trusted friend, doing a bit of research via a reliable online source (and the 'reliable' part is VERY important) or recalling some of your prior experiences of instincts-gone-wild and what the outcome actually was in those situations. If I bring to mind all the plane trips I've taken without incident – that'd be 100 per cent of them – it is easier for me to put my fears into perspective and understand that my feelings of impending doom are a function of my anxiety, rather than anything based in reality.

But there are some situations where you can't call a friend, do your research or reflect on your past experiences – say, when you feel you're being followed or the person you're with is a bit off, and in these moments, you should absolutely go with your gut. You need that little voice in your head telling you not to walk down the dark alley or amble towards the cliffs when you've had a few too many vodkas. When you're on unfamiliar turf, the landscape is foreign, your orientation is lousy and you are, at least to some degree, disinhibited and unshackled, like a foal but with a passport.

The ability to recognise danger is tremendously useful, if not essential, when you're travelling. You NEED to be able to recognise that getting into a Honda Civic with a self-styled shaman brandishing a 'talking feather' at 3am is a bad idea. Unfortunately, when this happened to me, I did NOT let my anxiety prevent me from getting in the car, and I spent the next 30 minutes trying to make peace with my own impending demise as the shaman ducked and weaved down the M4 at 200 miles per/hour. Eventually I told him I had a heart condition and needed him to slow down, which was not true, but would have been had I spent more time in his cosmic death sedan.

Having a higher level of resting anxiety is a neat way to avoid some of the pitfalls of being a tourist, and it's free. It is only when your instincts are impeding your ability to get out and live that you really need to call them into question.

Q&A
with
Casey Donovan

Singer/songwriter, actress and
R U OK? Ambassador

After winning Australian Idol at only 16 years old, Casey Donovan launched a celebrated career as an award-winning singer, screen and stage actor, writer, and presenter. She speaks openly about her own battles with anxiety and depression, and has for the last few years been a prominent ambassador for mental health awareness day, R U OK? Day.

At what age did you become conscious that your feelings of anxiety were a problem?

I think I've always had bouts of anxiety from a young age but didn't quite understand what it was until I was about 25 or 26. I was going to get a laser treatment and I was overwhelmed with what I didn't know at the time was anxiety. I became clammy, my heart was racing and I had a very uneasy feeling in the pit of my stomach.

How has your anxiety impacted your day-to-day life? Have you learned to recognise your triggers?

Anxiety impacts my day-to-day by sometimes stopping me in my tracks. If I'm getting ready to go out, I can be fine one minute and a bag of crying overwhelmed nerves the next.

I have learned to identify some of my triggers and sit with my anxiety, but learning how to do that didn't happen overnight. Some of my triggers were people talking about death, getting on planes (still battle that one), hearing about people having heart attacks ... death is a big trigger for me. Also, if I haven't slept enough, it can trigger my anxiety.

What are some of your red flags?

Anxiety can manifest in a thousand different ways. We might recognise what our triggers are, but find it more difficult to actually identify when we're spiralling. The biggest red flag for me is when I have to start repeatedly checking if my doors are locked and the stove is off – that's when I know I need to pay more attention to what's happening in my life, concentrate on my breathing and make sure I prioritise sleep, exercise and time with friends. Easier said than done!

Some things I notice when I am getting overwhelmed is my tendency to become introverted and not want to leave the house. I get a lot more jittery when I'm not looking after myself. Loss of sleep, agitation, mood swings and just wanting to be alone – that's when I know I need to stop and take a minute to ask myself what is going on.

You're obviously no stranger to travel. What do you like to do keep yourself calm on a plane?

I am not a great flyer but have to do it for my job. Sometimes I just jump on and I'm a great flyer and it's pain-free, but most of the time I am stressed and cannot relax. It's the 'getting there' that gives me anxiety, not so much the planning once I land. I'm not one for planning!

I have listened to so many podcasts on flying and being a nervous flyer, but somehow my irrational thoughts overpower me and I just sit there counting down the minutes. I can tell you how long it will take to fly anywhere, and before I have to do a long-haul flight, I look and see how long it's going to take and start to prepare myself. I know it's irrational and that my chances of dying in the air are small but when I am in the air, it all goes out the window.

Whilst I'm in the air, I try to do puzzles on my iPad or read until I fall asleep, sometimes I try to sleep whilst listening to a meditation.

What do you like to do when you arrive at your destination to feel settled and at home?

I'm usually just happy to be on the ground safely! So my anxiety is usually at bay and I'm so exhausted from stressing that I just try and get to my accommodation and get settled.

What do you think is the biggest upside to pushing through those anxious feelings and travelling?

The biggest upside is proving to myself that I can get on a plane and travel and fight my anxiety, and even sit with it and know that I am stronger than my mind and that everything will be okay.

CHAPTER THREE

Managing Anxiety

Anxiety is a many-tentacled octopus, encompassing
social phobias, germaphobia, obsessive-compulsive
disorder (OCD), panic disorders, general anxiety (GAD)
and post-traumatic stress disorder (PTSD) (*see* p.37). You
may have a diagnosis of GAD but still suffer symptoms of
OCD or panic disorder when your anxiety is particularly
high. You may have no official diagnosis of *anything* and
still suffer significant symptoms: Australian research
suggests less than half of people with anxiety disorders
seek diagnosis and treatment. Deciding to do so can
take years. This chapter helps explain how to manage
anxiety, find what works for you, and includes a Q&A
with psychologist Maggie Mazur (*see* p.38).

Lena Dunham nailed it when she said, 'We should be teaching kids from a young age that it's as okay to say "I'm anxious" as it is to say "I hit my knee"'. The earlier you get help, the better, but don't ever feel ashamed that you've left it too long – the reality is that lots of us just live uncomfortably alongside our anxiety until it becomes too big to ignore, like a grapefruit-sized psychic tumour.

Despite the fact that the first conscious thought I remember having as a child was 'I'm scared,' I did not acknowledge that anxiety was an issue for me until well into adulthood. Instead, I made being neurotic part of my personality and professional identity (which is fine when you're a writer, less so when you have a real job). There's nothing wrong with putting your frailties and quirks front and centre of your personality, of course – but it's wise to address and confront the things that actually make it distressing to be you, too. At some point, after all, you want your life to be something more than just a long-running gag. I waited until my life was indistinguishable from a Lars Von Trier film before finally committing to regular therapy, as well as all of the things that do not come naturally to me – like breathing deeply, exercising self-compassion and going to sleep at a reasonable hour.

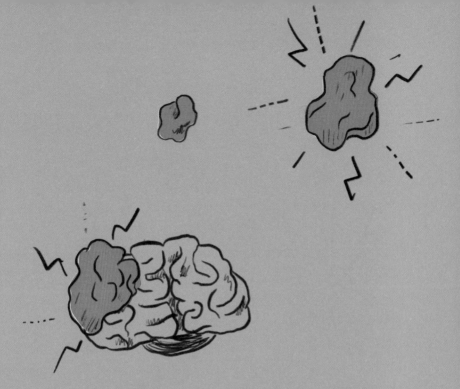

'Self-care' comes up a lot in discussions about managing anxiety, and while it doubtlessly plays a significant role in maintaining your physical and mental health, it's important to remember that self-care does not always function as a preventative, nor a cure, for anxiety. If we attach a lot of expectations to what self-care can do for our anxiety levels, it can create feelings of failure and disappointment when it doesn't work. Of course, walking, soaking in a bath and taking time to rest are useful relaxation tools, but when you're dealing with a major anxiety disorder, these kinds of measures may not be enough to ground you. It also sucks the joy out of simple pleasures: you are allowed to have baths, lie on the ground and stare at the clouds and go for walks without feeling obliged to make it an exercise in lowering your anxiety levels.

Being naturally idle and deeply concerned with my own comfort, I have never needed any encouragement to practice self-care; you don't have to ask me twice to soak in the tub or have a day nap. I do these things because I enjoy them, but they do not have any tangible impact on my OCD, germaphobia, and anxiety. In fact, when I go too far with the self-care measures (as happens quite often), I get lazy and unmotivated, which then makes me feel bad about myself, which in turn makes me anxious. So for me, working is often the treatment for, rather than the cause of, my anxiety. For others, the opposite holds true.

Find the things you love doing and do them because you want to, not because you feel you have to tick all the self-care boxes. Yoga, for instance. I have often felt like I should do yoga, as it's touted as a treatment for, well, everything, but despite trying it many, many times, I do not like it, and I do not want to do any more work on liking it. I have friends for whom it is invaluable though, but it's just not for me. On the other hand, roller-skating and self-hypnosis videos have a significant impact on how I'm able to manage my anxiety, as does dancing alone to very loud music and eating a lot of good food (never underestimate how nuts hunger can make you).

The ubiquitous advice to carve out regular blocks in our schedule for 'self-care' also assumes all of us live lives that permit us to regularly take time out. You may not be at a stage of your life where it's possible to spend a lot of time doing things for yourself. Remember, therapy and medication – often cited as the most effective combination in treating anxiety – is self-care too. The best approach is to talk to your medical professional and get their help on what will work for your needs.

Is my anxiety going to get worse when I travel?

The very thought of packing up your anxieties and taking them on holiday can seem like an invitation for an escalation in your anxiety, but most of the time, any worsening of symptoms you experience will be temporary. Most anxiety is anticipatory. Yes, you might feel more anxious before you go, but this is normal. Everybody – even people without anxiety disorders – feels anxious before they go away. We relinquish a lot of control when we travel, and must accept that things will sometimes go wrong. We have to open ourselves up to unpredictability (unless we're on a cruise but, for the sake of this book, let's say we're not).

In the days and weeks before you travel, think about what it is that's worrying you most. Identify your triggers. It may be the train or plane trip that's causing you the most anxiety, or the idea of being in a country where you can't speak the language. It may be that you're travelling solo for the first time. Or it may be the scramble to finish all your work before you go, or finding someone to feed your cat and collect your mail. Pinpointing your worries can help you better prepare for the parts of the journey you most fear.

If not speaking the language is your worry, ask yourself how many people you know who've died because they couldn't speak the language (I promise it will be *no one*). If the flight is worrying you, prepare a playlist of meditations to listen to on the flight, and find a calm breathing technique that you like. Pack an eye mask, some favourite snacks and books or magazines you've been wanting to read – anything you know that will provide a little mindless comfort and distraction.

You may have times when you feel so overwhelmed
with anxiety about your upcoming trip that you're
tempted to cancel. I know this feeling very well,
which is why I can tell you with some confidence:
PUSH IT AWAY. Your feelings of dread are your
anxiety speaking, not your instincts, not fate, not
your spiritual guardians. If you avoid the things
that frighten you, it can have the unintended
consequence of amplifying your anxiety. I have
plenty of regrets about travel opportunities I have
turned down, but none about any I have gone
ahead with.

A quick look at anxiety disorders

Obsessive-compulsive disorder (OCD)

Many people say they're 'a bit OCD', but there is a big difference between stacking your dishes a certain way, and suffering from actual obsessive-compulsive disorder (OCD). People with OCD experience intrusive or invasive anxiety-provoking thoughts, which they try to relieve with repetitive behaviours and rituals. For example, a fear of germs can cause someone to obsessively clean their hands, repeatedly count items, hoard, check the stove is off and the doors are locked. Despite rationally understanding that rituals or behaviours are unwarranted, it can be extremely difficult for people with OCD to break the cycle.

Generalised anxiety disorder (GAD)

No one cruises through life without breaking a nervous sweat from time to time but people with generalised anxiety disorder (GAD) feel anxious most of the time, which can severely impact their quality of life. Unlike phobias and

OCD, which centre around specific fears, GAD can create worries around daily life, from work, relationships and family, to finances and housing. A sense that something is always about to go wrong characterises GAD, along with physical symptoms such as headaches and stomach upsets. GAD can also lead to depression and other anxiety conditions, like social phobias.

Panic disorder

Everyone experiences high levels of anxiety at times because, well, life. About 5–10 per cent of people will experience a panic attack in their lives. Panic disorder – as opposed to occasional panic attacks – is characterised by recurrent panic attacks, the symptoms of which include chest pain, dizziness, palpitations, sweating and shortness of breath. Often, people think they're having a heart attack or dying and they have persistent fears of having another attack and believe that the symptoms are a sign of undetected medical problems – despite evidence to the contrary. Panic attacks usually peak after about ten minutes, and leave the person feeling exhausted and depleted.

Social phobia

Everybody lies awake some nights replaying all the dumb things they said at a party or worrying about all the dumb things they might say at work. But for people with social phobia, the fear of humiliation, embarrassment or being criticised is omnipresent.

Anxiety can be triggered by things like eating in public, small talk and asserting themselves. Physical symptoms can accompany social phobia, like excessive sweating, nausea, diarrhoea, palpitations, trembling, blushing and stuttering. People with social phobia often avoid situations where their fears may be realised, which can negatively impact their relationships and ability to function.

Post traumatic stress disorder

Post-traumatic stress disorder (PTSD) can sometimes occur after a person experiences a traumatic event, such as the loss of a loved one, assault or disaster. The condition was first observed in Vietnam War veterans, and since then a range of treatments have been developed which can dramatically improve the quality of life for people with PTSD, and many people fully recover. However some at-risk people, exposed to certain types of trauma, go on to suffer from PTSD or various other trauma-related conditions that have an anxiety component. Symptoms commonly include nightmares and flashbacks to the event, a tendency to be hyperalert to danger, irritability, an inability to concentrate, panic and extreme fear, and feelings of detachment from friends and family.

Q&A
with
Maggie Mazur

Psychologist (BA Psych, Master of Clinical Psychology)

What are some useful anxiety management techniques for people suffering a spike in their anxiety prior to travelling?

Travel anxiety is common and a degree of nervousness before new events, like travelling, is normal.

Anxiety is essentially a preoccupation with the future, with thoughts about things that are not happening and hence only exist in your mind. We run into trouble when these thoughts start turning into the anticipation of a wild range of catastrophic events and become a preoccupation. Worrying about our worries is like blowing into a fire. It can make the worries grow until we find ourselves overwhelmed by a worry inferno. Accepting that you're feeling anxious and trying to leave it at that will help to keep a lid on the worry box.

Managing travel anxiety starts with being realistic about where you're at with your anxiety, tailoring your trip to what you can handle, while being prepared to push yourself, and having strategies and supports in place. Pushing boundaries and doing things that make you uncomfortable will help you and is, in fact, an essential ingredient in overcoming anxiety.

Get help

Anxiety is highly treatable and the majority of people do improve with treatment, preferably from a registered psychologist or psychiatrist. If cost is an issue, in many countries there are free services. Chat to your doctor, search the net for local services or phone a mental health helpline to point you in the relevant direction.

Pay attention to your mind

Learn to pay attention to your mind and watch your thoughts without assigning any interpretations or judgements. With practice, you can learn to watch your thoughts float by without them impacting your mood. As you become more aware, you can start changing thoughts that pop up when you're anxious, to be more supportive, accepting and realistic. Once you have calmed down, you can try writing down the thoughts you had in particularly anxious moments. You can also write what is going through your mind during the moments of distress. This will provide a distraction and since writing is slower than thinking, it will help you talk yourself through your anxious thoughts and distance yourself from them.

Get in touch with your feelings

Work on noticing your feelings. People with anxiety have a tendency to supress their feelings, which in turn drives anxiety. Naming, expressing and communicating feelings is a learnt skill and a very important one in managing anxiety.

Put lifestyle practices in place

Are you getting good nutrition? Should you cut down on coffee, alcohol? Are you getting enough sleep? Little by little, swap that third coffee for a decaf, go to bed 20 minutes earlier, go for a walk just to the end of your street. Little changes are the key to forming new habits and make a big difference in the long run. Putting in a regular routine of physical exercise is particularly important.

Get a health check

It is worth having a chat with your doctor to rule out any physical issues. Anxiety is implicated in some physical conditions, for example, vitamin B12 deficiency, thyroid dysfunction and the sugar dips of diabetes. You will either find out that you're in tip-top shape, which will be great, or if something a bit amiss gets picked up, it can be fixed.

It might also be worthwhile to chat to your doctor about potential medication, as this may be a suitable option for you.

Identify your triggers

Learn to identify the specific thoughts, sensations or images that trigger your panic. When you are feeling calm and safe, sit and visualise the scenarios that make you panic (like getting on a plane, what you will hear and see, and all the other details), but instead of catastrophising, imagine feeling calm and imagine things going well.

Be prepared

A good way to manage when concerns are real, like during COVID, is to be as prepared as possible. As well as the usual travel planning, COVID means you have to keep up to date with the current situation in your destination and anywhere you are transitioning through.

Take control

You can control many practicalities of travel. For example, if you fear feeling closed in, book an aisle seat close to the exits or book a window seat if being able to see out will make you feel less claustrophobic. Build in extra time to get to the airport so you don't stress about every red light or getting a parking space. Give yourself enough time to sit down and have a coffee or a bit of calm time. Get some good rest before your trip, pack everything ahead and just have a relaxed day beforehand.

Learn to stay in the moment

Panic can often make you feel detached or separated from reality. Learning strategies that bring you into the present, like grounding techniques and tools that help you stay with your feelings without fighting them or being overwhelmed, will be helpful.

Breathe

Learn to manage your breathing. Consciously slowing down your breath has a physiologically calming effect, and when you persist it is a guaranteed way of calming yourself. Panic attacks often involve hyperventilation, and fearing the panic is what magnifies it. Consciously slow your breathing, making your out-breath longer than your in-breath. Count slowly to three as you breathe in, hold your breath for two, breathe out for five. Breathe in and out of your belly, focus on your abdomen expanding and deflating with each breath.

Relax

Muscle relaxation can also ease panic. Place your attention on your muscles. For example, starting with your hands, consciously tense them by making a fist and then relax, work through all the parts of your body, tensing and relaxing. Progressive muscle relaxation is one of the easiest to learn and there are plenty of free online guides.

Meditate

Meditation is an excellent tool for dealing with anxiety-provoking environments, like being on a plane or a bus. There are a wide range of meditation apps, podcasts and guided audio and video meditations, and many are free.

Get a toolbox of strategies

Learn strategies for dealing with distress in the moment. There are a range of things you can do to get through situations you find difficult. It is worth trying a whole lot of these ahead of travel to find what works best for you.

Preparing for Travel

This chapter will tell you how to prepare for travel, long before you ever begin your journey. When you begin to think about what to pack, what to research and where exactly to go, it's very easy to get overwhelmed, give up, go back to watching figure-skating highlights and spend the week before you go freaking out 24/7 about how ill-prepared you are. This is my usual approach. A better example is to follow the advice below, which, I swear, is what I will be doing before my next trip.

What to view and what not to view before you travel

To avoid serrating your nervous system before you travel, you must start modifying your behaviour well in advance of your trip.

Limit your consumption of the following 5 media

1. Any documentary that isn't about baby ducks or happily matrilineal societies

2. True crime shows/podcasts

3. Fake crime shows/podcasts

4. Social media

5. I'm not sure you were really paying attention – SOCIAL MEDIA

For anxious types (and doesn't social media, by design, make us ALL 'anxious types'?), Facebook and its extended family of social media platforms are like a field of beautiful sunflowers carpeted with landmines. 'I will just pop into that lovely field for a second to pick a flower/look for a backpack on Marketplace!' you say to yourself, and before you know it, you've stepped onto a landmine – an article about falling standards of plane maintenance, for example, or homicide rates

in Palermo. Instagram is comparatively benign, but it *will* give you unrealistic expectations about how consistently wonderful and photogenic your holiday will be, and encourage you to make the focal point of your trip photographing it for a wider audience rather than enjoying it for yourself.

Limit your media consumption to streaming services, where you can tightly control what you see. Choose shows your parents – no, your *grandma* – would enjoy. *Golden Girls*, *The Crown*, *Downton Abbey*, *Escape to the Country*, *Antiques Roadshow*. Teen films made in the '80s and '90s do the job nicely, too – think *Pretty in Pink, Ferris Bueller's Day Off* and *Clueless*.

Temporarily unfollow hard news pages and friends who get off on doom-posting. Living in a state of wilful ignorance is, under ordinary circumstances, not to be recommended. But when you're about to do something terrifying, like go on a holiday, it is wholly necessary. (However, frustrating as it is, in the age of the COVID pandemic, keeping up with the news about where you're headed to is prudent. Travellers will need to check lockdowns, social restrictions and vaccination requirements.)

Wise and sensible things that you really need to do before you travel

On occasion, I have become so overwhelmed with broad-spectrum travel anxiety that I have completely lost sight of the basic safety and security issues – like taking out travel insurance, giving a couple of trusted people my itinerary, and making sure I have the correct credit and debit cards to travel with. Instead, I've maintained a myopic focus on one comparatively small aspect of the trip (that bloody toiletries bag, *see* p.69 if you have the same problem).

Do these 5 things before you go

1.

Sort out your passport and visas

If travelling overseas, make sure you have a passport (*see* p.61) and check the visa requirements within each country you're planning on visiting, as it's a requirement of entry in many countries. Allow plenty of time for this, as some visas take a long time to process.

2.

Research the hell out of your destination

This doesn't mean 'book the hell out of your destination'. The more familiar you are with where you're going (how the public transport works, where the best place to stay is, how to say at least a few greetings in the local language), the faster you'll find your feet once you arrive. By research, I mean reading guidebooks by people who have spent coveted amounts of time in Venice or New York. Social media can be a useful research tool too, as long as you keep in mind that some travel accounts present sanitised, rose-tinted versions of reality. Make sure any accommodation you book has plenty of verified reviews and is easily accessible on foot or via public transport.

3.
Get a health check

Do this at least six to 12 weeks before you leave and make sure you're up to date with any vaccinations or boosters needed for travel (*see* p.54).

4.
Take out travel insurance

There is a chance you'll require some sort of medical help or incur delay-related costs, and without travel insurance you'll be – what's the English word for it? – stuffed. Do this at least 15 days in advance of your trip and read the fine print so if there's an emergency, you know what you're covered for. Also, keep a copy of your travel insurer's phone number and your

policy number separate to your luggage – a copy in your hand luggage and checked-in baggage is a good idea.

There's an old and wise saying that says if you can't afford travel insurance, you can't afford to travel.

5.
Check your luggage allowance

Check the luggage allowances with each airline you'll be using. You do not want to face the crushing predicament of having to choose between your duty-free bottle of Bombay Sapphire or boarding your flight.

(And make sure you can easily carry your own bags. It's one thing to lift them off your bedroom floor, but another when you're running late for a train and have to hightail along a platform and climb up steps to a carriage lugging a 30kg suitcase).

Shine and polish your earthly vessel prior to travel

In simpler terms, book an appointment with your doctor and make sure you're up to date with your vaccinations.

One moment you're ambling through life, pleasantly alert and engaged, when suddenly you begin to feel wretchedly fatigued, and not just because you took melatonin then sabotaged its efficacy by reading the *Daily Mail* on your phone till 3am. You go to the doctor and get a full blood examination, which reveals your iron levels are on the slender side. You book in for an infusion, wait six weeks for the effects to take hold and in the meantime use your crummy ferritin count as an excuse to eat double cheeseburgers for lunch every day. Easy.

But not so easy if the fatigue suddenly hits when you're attempting to walk the Camino, which is why it is essential to get a full health check at least six to 12 weeks before you leave. Make sure you're up to speed with any vaccinations you'll need, as different countries have different vaccination requirements. At the time of writing,

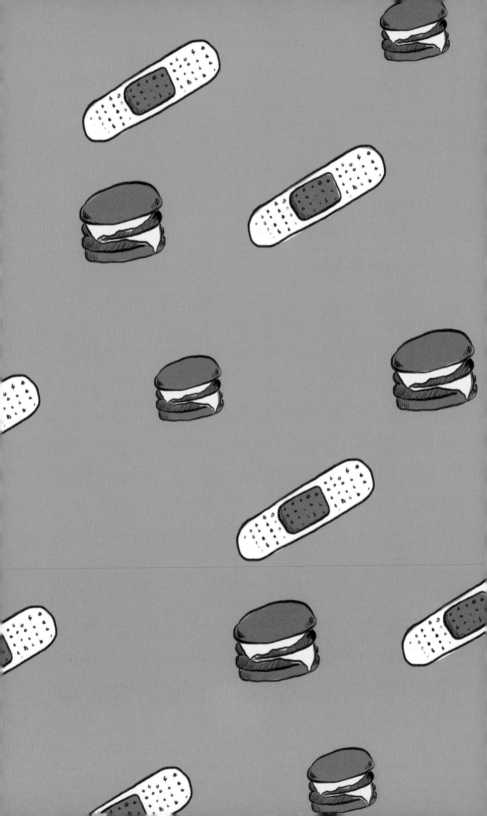

for example, it seems likely that most countries will soon require proof of a COVID-19 vaccination on entry. You may also be at higher risk of picking up infections such as measles, mumps, rubella, diptheria, tetanus, whooping cough, polio, and flu in certain places, so make sure you are up to date with your boosters. Vaccines prevent two to three million deaths per year. If you're looking for more detailed information, check government sites, like Smart Traveller in Australia (smarttraveller.gov.au), the US travellers' health section of the US Centre for Disease Control and Prevention (wwwnc. cdc.gov/travel and the UK's Travel Health Pro (travelhealthpro.org.uk).

It's also very important to take a prescription for any medications you regularly require and get your doctor to write a letter explaining what each medication is used for, as many countries have different laws around the sale and use of different medications. What's over the counter where you live may be a banned substance in another. It may seem like a lot to take in, but if you book an appointment with your doctor well in advance of your departure date and talk it all through with them, you'll be well prepared for your trip, and up to speed with everything you need to do on the health front.

On the day of your trip

Oof. There is no way around this: you will have enough nervous energy on the day you depart to power a nuclear reactor. Yes, you can do breathing exercises and visualisations and meditation, but you're still going to have a heart that thumps at double its normal rate. That's okay. Remember, the most nerve-wracking aspect of travel is usually the anticipation of travel rather than actually travelling. Airports are thrumming hives of nervous anticipation. Nobody, apart from the jaded corporates for whom daily plane commuting is par for the course, doesn't feel at least a twinge of anticipatory anxiety at the airport. I have dropped friends off at the airport for weekend trips interstate and still felt my stomach rumble with that very specific mix of excitement and fear.

Do these 5 things on the day of your trip

1.

Set your alarm

Wake up two hours prior to the time you need to leave your home. This gives you plenty of time to pack any last-minute items, eat and charge your phone and any other devices.

2.

Eat

If you can manage it, try and choke down a banana and a couple of pieces of toast – the banana will give you a hit of calming magnesium, which also helps regulate the heartbeat, and the toast will helpfully soak up excess stomach acid and provide good fats and carbs to see you through until your next meal.

3.

Confirm your flight or train is departing on schedule

Check ahead of time that your plane, train or bus is running on time. This will save you a dull couple of hours staring listlessly at a donut kiosk on account of a delay or cancellation.

4.

Don't shower until the very last minute

You're likely to spend a fair bit of time rushing around in a state of mild panic and sweating up a storm while you double-check everything's ready to go. But do take a shower – you'll feel infinitely better starting your journey clean and fresh.

5.

Give a set of keys to a trusted local friend or neighbour

This way you can't accidentally lock yourself out while something essential, like your phone or passport, remains trapped inside. It also means someone can check on your place to make sure it hasn't become pop-up accommodation for homeless snakes or rodents.

Passport anxiety-reduction tip

Ah, the passport. The most valuable, non-negotiable travel accessory if you are crossing international borders. Passports are so important that it feels like they should be much, much bigger, ergo much harder to lose, like a surfboard. No surfer has ever accidentally left her board under the seat in the transit lounge.*

In the absence of a surfboard-sized passport, make sure you have a special pocket for it in your bag or backpack that is both able to be zipped shut and easily accessed with one hand. If it can't be zipped closed, the likelihood of it falling into the Bermuda Triangle of the rest of your bag is 100 per cent. Take a photograph of the front page to store in your phone, and a put a photocopy in your luggage. It's also a very good idea to leave a copy with someone reliable back home, in case (God forbid) your luggage is stolen. Your passport should be valid for at least six months before you enter another country, but some airlines require your passport to be valid for six months from the date you *return* home.

Travel writer and journalist Larissa Dubecki, a nervous traveller herself, has a useful strategy to keep her 'shit-where's-my-passport?!' phobia under control. She says: 'I used to check every minute that it was still in the bag and hadn't magically been lost. I now allow myself 10 emergency passport checks each flight, so I have to dole them out sensibly rather than going in one huge hit just in the taxi on the way to the airport.'

*unverified

CHAPTER FIVE

To PacK
or not to
PacK

Nobody ever said, 'Thank God I brought those cotton wool balls!' while standing under the Eiffel Tower ... Aka, do not pack cotton wool balls or anything else you do not routinely use. For more information about why you never need cotton wool balls for anything EVER, *see* p.72.

Toiletries bag

My travel philosophy until quite recently could best be summed up as: 'nothing can go wrong if you pack enough drugs with the word 'anti' in them'. Antibiotics, antihistamines, antiemetics, anti-anxieties, anti-diarrhoea tablets: my toiletries bag looked like it had been packed by Michael Jackson's anaesthetist and Judy Garland's pharmacist.

In addition to the hefty stash of anti-sick pills, I would also pack Chinese herbal tinctures, probiotic pills, prebiotic pills, ginger pastilles, mint chews, and vitamin powders. Then there was all the face stuff: make-up, moisturisers, cleansers, toning masks, exfoliating masks, calming masks, hydrating masks, brightening masks, repairing masks, and age-defying masks, none of which I ever use at home – much less on holiday.

In 2017, I set off on what was intended to be a six-week European vacation with my partner and kids, but which in fact became an involuntary study tour of the health care systems of Singapore, Italy, and Germany. The details are boring, unless you have a special interest in gastroenterology (which, in my experience, even gastroenterologists do not really have). All you need to know is that it started with diarrhoea on a plane, and it ended with diarrhoea on a plane. My oldest daughter spent four days in a Sicilian hospital, and it was there, staring forlornly at the tawdry little courtyard garden outside her window while trying to untangle my anus from the wodge of sticky blue vinyl upon which I had been seated for 72 hours, that I realised not every catastrophe can be averted with a nicely packed toiletries bag.

That's not to say you should travel with only the clothes on your back and a hopeful disposition. You just shouldn't need to hire a shipping container to transport your bags to your destination.

Forgo packing any toiletries that can't save your life, or at least make your death a bit less painful. Ginger pastilles are no defence against a tidal wave of puke (trust me), and lavender oil is *not* sufficiently calming to take the edge off a missed flight or slight misunderstanding with the Sicilian mafia over the appropriate bin to put used nappies in. Homeopathic tinctures will not bring down a 40-degree fever (who, but me in 2017, did not already know this?).

But most importantly, overzealous packing of your toiletries bag leaves no room for one of life's greatest pleasures: bringing home shampoo and soaps from foreign pharmacies. My favourite travel memory is not of seeing the Colosseum for the first time, marvelling at the beauty of a Tuscan sunset or eating a still-warm baguette in the 7th arrondissement in Paris. My favourite travel memory is of spending an entire day filling my shopping basket with toothpaste, soap and sunscreen at the drogerie markt (drug store) in Berlin. *This*, I thought to myself as I cycled back to our apartment, *is what travel is really about. Flying to the other side of the world to stock up on toothpaste with labels you can't read.*

So, what can I take?

It's always a good idea to take two toiletries bags: a bigger one for the non-essentials to go in your checked-in baggage and a little bag to go in your carry-on, with all the stuff that would induce a coronary incident were the airline to accidentally lose the bigger one.

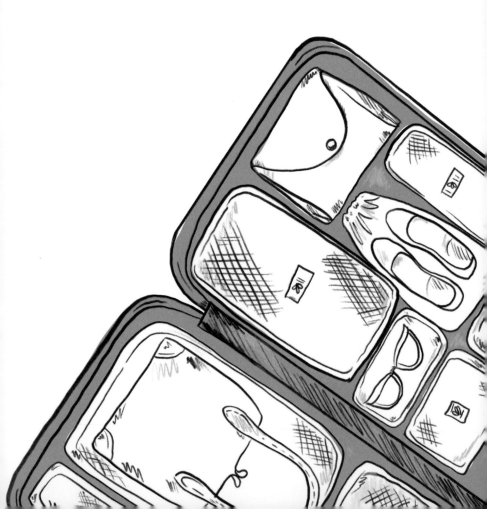

BIG
toiletries
bag

- Travel-size shampoo and conditioner – enough to last three days.

- Travel-size body wash.

- Pads and tampons/period underwear/ menstrual cup. Take a few in your carry-on, just in case, and a box of tampons or pads in your checked baggage. It can be surprisingly hard to find a brand that you like when you're away. Italians, for example, do almost everything better than anyone else in the world – bread, fashion, airports, floating cities – but they make terrible menstrual products.

- A box of paracetamol/acetaminophen / ibuprofen for headaches/period pain, if this something you have taken before and know you tolerate well.

- Hairbrush or comb.

- Any non-essential make-up and beauty products.

- Birth control.

- Sunscreen.

LITTLE
toiletries
bag

- Ear plugs.

- A small amount of paracetomol/acetaminophen/ ibuprofen (if you have used it before and know you have no adverse reaction).

- Hand sanitisers (two – one always rolls under your seat, never to be seen again).

- Travel-size disinfecting wipes.

- Surgical or reusable face masks.

- Hair ties, bobby pins – more than you think you could ever possibly need.

- Lip balm.

- Cleansing face wipes.

- Cotton wool pads, which serve a multitude of purposes.

- Moisturising cream, oil, or spritz for your hands and face.

- Mini dry shampoo. Everything dries out on planes, except for your hair; your hair will look like tempura by the end of your flight.

- Toothpaste and toothbrush. Your teeth are the only body part you can wash at 30,000 feet, and by the end of the flight you'll be pretty desperate for some part of you to feel fresh and clean.

- Medication. This is one area in which you can let your anxiety go off-leash. If you're an asthmatic who hasn't had an asthma attack for six months, put your puffer in your carry-on. If you experience occasional panic attacks, make sure you have anti-anxiety medication in your carry-on. You don't need to plan for every health scenario, just the ones that you've had recent experience with. Make sure you have a letter from your doctor detailing any prescription medications. Visit your doctor before you travel (*see* p.54).

- Make-up (if you wear it). You will find that you wear less make-up on holidays, especially if it's a good one. You will get so caught up in your new surrounds, you'll forget that society/Instagram expects you to always look like you've just had a snail mucus facial and multiple orgasms.

- Band-Aids of varying sizes. As much as I love drug store shopping, hobbling about for three hours trying to find blister coverings is not to be recommended.

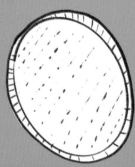

You do not need ...

- Cotton wool balls. No one ever needs cotton wool balls for anything. It's a mystery as to why they weren't just fazed out once cotton wool pads were invented.

- Super-sized supplies of anything. Remember, you're going to buy the entire contents of a German drug store.

- A mirror. Your phone is a mirror.

- Any make-up that you don't use on a daily or at *least* weekly basis.

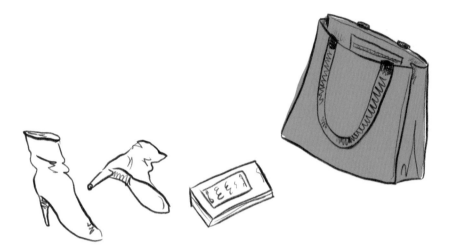

How to
pack
clothes

Squirrels hoard nuts just in case they run out, which they never do. The human equivalent of this is trying to stuff your whole wardrobe into a suitcase, just in case you encounter flood, fire, snow, sleet, scorching heat or punishing cold. It is important to push through this urge, as you will wear the same two outfits for the entirety of your trip, whether it be for six days or six months. Pack three comfortable outfits that never fail you. Don't take a winter coat to the Bahamas 'just in case'.

Sample list of essential wardrobe items:

- Walking shoes that fit properly, plus one other pair of shoes, two max. If you're hitting a few different climates, you may want to bring sandals and boots in addition to walking shoes.

- Swimwear, sarong/kaftan. Always bring swimwear no matter the climate you're visiting – you never know when you may be tempted to take a dip.

- One jacket, one cardigan, and one sweater for keeping warm – the best-quality ones you have. If you can afford cashmere or buy it second-hand, it is the most lightweight yet warm fabric on earth, and it feels like Persian kittens.

- No more than two T-shirts and two long-sleeve tops, two pairs of trousers or skirts, and two pairs of shorts. A good rule of thumb is no more than two of anything, except underwear and socks.

- A 'good' outfit for going out.

- One set of sleep clothes. I usually just take a pair of sleep shorts and an extra T-shirt than can do double duty as a sleep top and a day top.

- A week's supply of underpants and two bras, if you choose to wear them.

- Three pairs of socks. If you're only visiting warm climates, you can get away with one or two, although it is nice to wear socks on flights.

- A large wrap or scarf that can double as a blanket on planes, trains, and buses.

- If it's a ski holiday or any other kind of specialist holiday, you'll obviously have extra gear to pack, so your list of essentials may look a bit different.

A note on shoes

Never take new shoes without first breaking them in at home. Even the daintiest pair of sandals can become instruments of torture when you haven't yet put in the required hours of break-in time, and you do not want your memories of seeing a Galapagos turtle for the first time marred by the fact that your feet feel like they've been soaked in sulphuric acid. Trust me, man. The humble blister may not rank up there with childbirth or a broken bone, but it is a ruthlessly efficient joy killer, nonetheless. I once wound up in *hospital* on account of an infected toe blister. It was only for two hours, and at no point was I required to wear a white gown, but it was an embarrassing and painful interlude, and I have never again taken new shoes on holidays without first breaking them in.

Unusual, yet very useful tip

Rose Bessette, a seasoned traveller who works as a researcher in sexual health – aka knows a thing or two about vaginas – advises wearing multiple panty liners on a long-haul trip. During a flight, your vagina can fall prey to the combined effects of nerves (sweat) and poor ventilation. The poor dear doesn't get much in the way of breathing space. This can result in an uncomfortably swamp-like feeling in your knickers, and you don't really want to be burning through your entire supply of underwear on one flight, nor trying to change it every two hours in the dollhouse-coffin confines of the airplane toilet. Rose's genius solution means that every time things get too damp for comfort, you simply go to the toilet and peel off your panty liner to reveal a fresh one underneath.

You could also just take a pack of panty liners and keep changing them, one at a time, rather than piling them on top of one another like a feminine hygiene layer cake, but I appreciate the pragmatic laziness of Rose's suggestion. Go for supersize ... Dreamliner size, let's call them, so that any – how can I say this nicely – *ass sweat* is also captured.

Documents, devices and cash

Print booking confirmations and store them in a purse or plastic pocket for easy, wireless access. The less dependent you are on your phone, the better, as phones have a tendency to fall in toilets, run out of battery and get left on cafe tables.

Pack your own powerboard, and that way you'll only need one international adaptor to charge all your devices when you arrive.

Take some local currency in cash wherever you go; you can exchange it at the airport on departure, in case it's hard to find a currency exchange place on arrival. Sometimes you'll arrive at a time of day when currency exchanges are closed too, so keep this in mind. Not all businesses the world over take cards – think markets and street stalls – and you don't always want to use a card if you're just purchasing a drink. And if you're carrying more than one currency, keep them separate so you don't get confused and accidentally pay a taxi driver euros instead of dirhams.

Snacks for travel

Pack lots of snacks in your day pack or carry-on (but check beforehand what you can take through customs), as it's unwise to depend on the food provided on your flight or train, especially if you suffer with food intolerances or allergies. Even if you have pre-ordered a special meal in advance, it's not uncommon for these to accidentally wind up in someone else's hands, and belly.

Even if you don't have food allergies, taking plenty of healthy snacks on the journey is a wise idea, as plane and train food has a justifiably poor reputation. Personally I quite enjoy it, capsicum (red pepper) dip food poisoning incident notwithstanding, but I have a generous appetite and rarely find the servings big enough. I always pack extra snacks to get me through – dried apple, rice crackers, and nuts.

If you'll be flying, it's worth noting there is a school of thought that says you should eat very lightly in the air, as the altitude negatively impacts your digestion, but how hung up on being virtuously healthy do you want to be when you're on holiday? There isn't much to do on a plane but eat and sleep, so if you're hungry, *eat*.

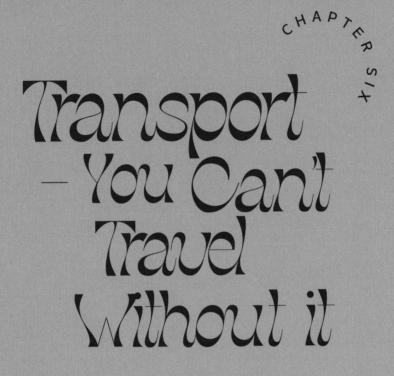

CHAPTER SIX

Transport – You Can't Travel Without it

Helicopters, light aircraft, skyrails, speedboats, hot-air balloons – all have the capacity to induce anxiety, but for the purposes of this chapter, we're just going to look at planes (*see* p.82), trains (*see* p.92), boats (*see* p.96), and buses (*see* p.100), as I think it's safe to assume very few of us intend to use a hot-air balloon as our primary mode of transport. This chapter will help you navigate transport and give you some helpful tips. A pilot shares her expert tips for flying (*see* p.84) and helps alleviates our fears.

Flying is not normal unless your home is a nest

A fear of flying, in particular, can really mess with your plans and even tempt you to ditch them altogether, but if you want to visit the Greek Islands or catch a performance at the Lincoln Centre, you're going to need to find a way to push through those fears.

Let's get one thing straight: humans do not have wings, and that is all you need to know to understand why so many of us want to puke during take-off. Our bodies are not built for *taking off*. The only people who feel 100 per cent fine with flying are touring musicians (because they're drunk) and the flight crew (because even bungee-jumping off Everest ceases to be frightening if you do it every day).

Being mild to moderately scared of flying is very common, but that doesn't make it any more tolerable for the sufferer. Take heart: a slew of studies exist to demonstrate just how unlikely it is that your worst fears will be realised. For instance, a US National Transportation Safety Board (NTSB) review revealed the startling fact that, of all the aircraft accidents between 1983 and 1999, 95 per cent of passengers survived, and even in the most serious incidents, 55 per cent of the occupants survived. In the years since the NTSB study was conducted, flying has only gotten safer. A cursory glance at transport statistics reveals that flying is by far the safest way to travel. If we were as concerned about road safety statistics as we are about air safety statistics, we would never set foot in a car.

And if you're worried that in the wake of COVID-19, pilots who haven't been able to fly throughout 2020/21 will be a little less sure of themselves in the cockpit, pilot Libby Bakewell, who you'll meet in a moment, reports that all grounded pilots will be spending about three to four months updating and consolidating their skills, both in flight simulators and in the air, before they're permitted to fly passenger jets again.

Q&A
with
Libby Bakewell

Pilot and Aviation Safety Specialist

Libby Bakewell is a commercial pilot, aviation safety expert and former flight attendant. Libby also used to work on Qantas's fear of flying course, and she was a crew member on board a hijacked TAA flight from Perth to Melbourne in 1983. It was this incident that sparked Libby's interest in the human factors at play in aviation safety. She knows more about flying than you and I and almost everyone else in the world, and she's not remotely scared of it, which I find very reassuring – like someone who's been to hell coming back and reporting that 'Actually, it's not that hot'.

How can we increase our odds of surviving a plane crash?

Most people don't realise that their chances of survival are largely dependent on how they behave and how they've prepared. You need to watch the safety demonstration, listen to the audio announcements and read the safety card every single time you fly, no matter how often.

Evacuations often take place in the dark so count how many seats between you and the nearest exit, as you have to assume that you won't be able to see.

Don't drink too much. You will not be in a position to act quickly if you're affected by alcohol. Evacuations are designed to take place within 90 seconds; that's how long it should take to completely evacuate a plane. Your reaction times are just not going to be quick enough if you've had a few wines. Sleeping pills can also impair your ability to deal with an emergency situation too.

It's also extremely important to leave your carry-on luggage in the overhead locker when you're evacuating. It dramatically slows down the evacuation and congests the aisles – all it takes is one person to trip and fall over, or for bags to end up blocking an exit during an evacuation. Trying to retrieve your carry-on in an emergency situation will cost lives.

I always stow a little purse (with a strap that goes across the body to make it hands-free) with my passport, phone, wallet, and keys in the compartment with the safety card and magazines – that way I can just grab that little purse if I need to evacuate without wasting any time or impeding my mobility (or anyone else's) with a carry-on bag.

Which part of the flight is the most dangerous?

Definitely take-off and landing. But the chances of anything happening are still extremely low. Cabin crew, whether flying on duty or off, *always* assume a modified brace position during take-off and landing – with their hands placed palms-down on their legs, their feet firmly on the ground, and their chin tilted. If facing forward, your chin should be tilted slightly downward. If facing backward, then your head should be back against the headrest with your chin tilted slightly up. This is only for a period of about twenty seconds, so you would never notice it – but we all do it.

One of my other best safety tips for take-off and landing is to keep your shoes on – if there is an emergency situation, you will need them to protect your feet and help get you quickly away from the plane, even though you may need to temporarily take them off if you evacuate via the slides. Never wear high heels – they make it much more difficult to move quickly, and if you are evacuating a plane, you're probably going to need to run away from it as fast as you can once you disembark.

Can turbulence cause the plane to crash?

No. The planes are built to withstand turbulence. We have radars that show us if we're going to enter an area of extreme turbulence, and we can go around it. However, not all turbulence can be detected on the radar, and that's why you should keep your seatbelt on as much as is practically possible. Planes don't crash because of turbulence, but people can be seriously injured if the plane hits clear air turbulence, which doesn't show on the radar, and they don't have their seatbelts on.

It's an embarrassing question, but one I ask on behalf of almost everyone I know: how on earth does this hulking great lump of machinery loaded with human cargo actually stay in the air?

It's all about air pressure. A simple way to think about it is to think about what happens when you stick your hand out the window of a moving car – if you hold your hand at an angle, it will create lift (which just means there's more pressure on one side than the other), and your hand will rise.

The actual engines of the aircraft don't create lift and they don't lift the weight at all – they simply push the aircraft forward, and the motion of the air over the wings creates the lift. What that means is that if the engines were to suddenly fail, your plane would still continue to glide perfectly well for some time, using the huge potential energy of the aircraft's altitude.

And finally, what are your best tips for staying calm while flying?

Mindfulness, meditation, diaphragmatic breathing – all those things are really helpful. Lots of crew fly with essential oils for sleep and relaxation. The crew also tend to fill their hot water bottles during breaks to help them relax and get to sleep more easily. Passengers won't necessarily be able to do this, but you could bring a couple of those portable heat packs in your carry-on.

Having a really thorough understanding of how flying works, and just how many layers of safety are built into every part of the journey, is very helpful in overcoming a fear of flying. Knowing, for instance, that the plane makes a lot of noises, and none of them signal doom – people forget that passenger jets are loaded with all kinds of cargo, and while it's all safely secured, it still moves! The wings make noise, the landing gears makes noises. Those bells that you always hear are simply crew communicating with each other – a routine part of every flight.

Train travel evokes romance

Shanghai Express, Murder on the Orient Express, The Girl on the Train – train travel as depicted in books and films frequently evokes a heady atmosphere of romance, crime, and intrigue, conveniently overlooking the fact that, most of the time, train travel is simply standing in an overcrowded carriage on your way to work and quietly vomiting into your hand as the person next to you noisily masticates an egg and bacon roll.

But *holiday* train travel is an opportunity to see the romantic side of it, the kind that involves dreamily staring out the window as mile after mile of ever-changing scenery unfurls before you. Train travel makes the journey part of the holiday, rather than simply a means of delivering you to your destination. In many countries, train travel affords you glimpses of the most remarkable scenery, landmarks and national parks, which cannot be said for plane travel. Train travel is also one of the most eco-friendly options, using less energy than both cars and planes.

Train travel is a good alternative for nervous flyers, having the distinct advantage of bypassing the stress of airport queues and lengthy transit times, and as a general rule offering a higher degree of comfort than plane travel. Train stations in Europe, for example, are usually located in the centre of the town or city, which removes another somewhat stressful aspect of travel from the equation – getting to an airport, which are usually located some distance from a city.

Tips for travelling by train

- Make sure you do plenty of research in advance of your trip if you'd like to make train travel a part of your holiday.

- Fares can vary wildly depending on how far in advance of your journey you book them, whether or not you're buying tickets in a group and what kind of rail pass you're using.

- Train services can vary wildly too, even within the same country, so check if you're on an express or a stopping at all stations service.

- If you're travelling overnight, you might want to spend the money on a sleeper train or compartment that will give you comfort and some privacy.

- If you're on a long train journey in a country where you don't speak the language, show the conductor your ticket so they can let you know in advance which stop to get off at.

- Although train travel is a far more leisurely affair than plane travel, you should still stick to the same basic principles: get to the station at least 30 minutes in advance of your trip, keep all your valuables on you at all times (a small backpack will do – this way can you move easily between carriages without worrying about your stuff) and bring disinfecting wipes to clean taps, trays and even toilets before you use them.

- Take food and water on board too, even for short trips (in case of delays), and even if trains have onboard catering you never know what you'll get served.

- While it's not the end of the world if you get sick on holiday, continuing with the simple hygiene precautions we're all so well versed in because of COVID will give you the best chance of avoiding a holiday bug.

There may not be cruises, but there will be boats

I'll be honest. If you are reading this book, it's unlikely cruise ship holidays are on your radar. They are not the natural habitat of the anxious young traveller. I used to write advertising material for cruise ship operators, and none of my professional touting of the benefits of cruising did anything to shake my personal belief that travelling via pelican beak would be preferable to travelling via cruise ship. Cruise ships are notorious super-spreader settings, not just for COVID but for gastroenteritis – bad news if, like me, you suffer from emetephobia (fear of vomiting).

Cruise ships are also rarely the correct choice for the more introverted or reflective traveller who values plenty of personal space and wants to leave room for idle wanderings in their itinerary. To be fair, many people genuinely adore travelling on cruise ships, but while the average age of the cruise ship traveller is starting to skew younger, they are still most popular with seniors. Younger people who enjoy cruises tend to be professional party animals, whose DNA is shaped like the party hat and streamers emoji rather than the double helix. If you try to keep up with the professional party animals on a cruise, you will need a liver transplant by day 10. You are better advised to stick to planes, trains and the odd boat ride across Lake Como.

'The only sure cure for sea sickness is to sit under a tree,' comedian Spike Milligan once said, but sitting under a tree is not always a realistic option when you're on holiday. Certain destinations are more difficult, if not impossible, to get to or to see properly via any other means of transport. In Sydney, for instance, you miss out on a lot, not to mention deal with a lot more traffic, if you forgo the city's iconic ferries.

Tips for travelling by boat

- If you're worried about motion sickness, carry some strong mints or ginger lollies in your bag to help quell the nausea. Don't eat or drink too much before the ride.

- Stand with your legs further apart than usual and keep your eyes fixed on the horizon – both tried-and-true mariner methods of helping your body adjust to the motion of the sea.

- If you're not used to being on boats and are feeling nervous about sea sickness, practice your favourite variation on calm breathing during the ride.

- If you have a history of severe motion sickness, talk to your doctor before you leave, as you may feel more comfortable with an emergency supply of anti-nausea medication in your backpack.

- If you are scared of travelling via boat, it can be hard to find the kind of reassuring data readily available to nervous flyers, as comprehensive records of marine deaths are difficult to locate, but know this: casualty estimates between the years 2000 to 2012 run from around 300 to 644. You are more likely to die in the cab on the way to port rather than on the boat itself.

- As with plane travel, familiarise yourself thoroughly with all the safety and evacuation procedures before the journey begins.

Bus travel means you can chat to the locals

Bus travel offers many of the benefits of train travel, minus the romantic mythology, but at a much lower cost. Like train travel, bus travel is both an eco-friendly choice, with a much lower rate of accidents and fatalities than car travel, and a convenient one, with depots and stations generally located in city centres rather than on the outskirts of towns.

One of the biggest advantages of choosing bus travel is that you don't have to do a lot of research into the cheapest fares, nor put a lot of thought into how far in advance you need to book, as bus fares don't tend to change according to when you book, and they are frequently on sale. Tickets can often be booked online, requiring you to only scan your QR code on boarding, and cancellation policies are much more flexible than most airline carriers.

Many buses now also come equipped with wi-fi and electrical sockets. You can sit and listen to music or read, and bus travel means you can chat to the locals or to other travellers.

As with train and air travel, you'll need to make sure you have a small bag or backpack in addition to your hand luggage for storing your money, passport, and phone and anything else you could not bear to part with.

Tips for travelling by bus

- Make sure you research how long it takes to get from your accommodation to the bus station so you're able to build this into your schedule. Plan to arrive at the bus station a minimum of 15 minutes in advance of the departure time.

- Find out whether you need to book tickets in advance or whether you can buy them at the station or from the driver.

- Check if seating is allocated so you can book a seat in your preferred spot on the bus beforehand.

- Check if the bus has a toilet, how often it stops and whether or not you're permitted to disembark to stretch your legs and grab a snack during any stops.

- Take an eye mask for day naps, as buses are generally very bright.

- Load up your devices with your favourite podcasts, and pack books and magazines in your daypack, as not every bus will have onboard entertainment options.

- Keep your valuables with you at all times (in a bag that can either cross over your body or you can keep on your lap – some people even put them under their clothes) and never leave them unattended.

- Pack plenty of snacks and water.

- Wear clothing you can layer, as buses are usually air conditioned and can get very cold.

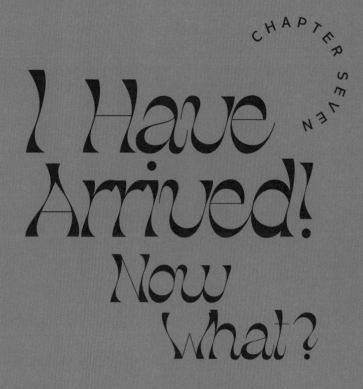

I Have Arrived! Now What?

CHAPTER SEVEN

Let's go ahead and say your train or plane did not crash, as this is one of the few safe assumptions we can make about your trip. So, let's say you're at the airport, you've watched your YouTube terminal guides (or looked at the directional signage) and you have an approximate idea of how to get from one end of the place to the other. You have also decided in advance which mode of transport you'll take to your hotel or hostel because this is a decision you do not want to be making when you've just dragged your carcass off a long flight.

In fact, you do not *ever* want to be making *any* decisions at the airport. Trying to make decisions at the airport is like trying to decide what to eat for dinner while having root canal work. Airports are the wrong environment for making any decision beyond which breathless gossip magazine to purchase at the newsagent (newsstand); I always choose *HELLO!* for its relentlessly jaunty reportage of the least important events in the world ('DIAMOND DUCHESS DAZZLES ON DATE NIGHT WITH WILLIAM').

Knowing well in advance how you plan to get from the airport to your accommodation will save you a lot of headaches, as every airport offers its own bewildering smorgasbord of transport options, some well-priced and reliable, others less so.

I'm at the hotel! My holiday has begun!

Next, we're going to assume you've made it in one happy, bedraggled heap to your accommodation. If you've been on a long-haul flight or travelling all day, you cannot lie down for an hour, no matter how loudly and persistently your body implores you to do so. If you lie down, you will fall asleep and wake up 12 hours later, entombed in your own dried saliva, desperate for a pizza. Being 3am, you will not be able to find one, and this, more so than any sensible ideas about re-setting your circadian rhythms, is the best reason I can think of to fend off the urge to sleep. Go get the pizza NOW. Do not think, 'I'll just set my alarm and rest for 15 minutes!'. Unless your alarm has a gloved-fist mechanism that punches you in the face when it goes off, it will *not* succeed in waking you.

If you're in a new time zone, try and stay up until at least 8.30pm the first night, 9pm the second, and by day three or four your body should begin to adjust to the new time zone. The thought is that every one hour of time difference equates to one day of jet lag, and anecdotally it seems to carry some weight – bad news for travellers from Australia and New Zealand, who generally fly into time zones many, many hours behind their own. It's a good idea to factor in a few days of jet lag when you're planning your schedule, as launching into full-scale tourist activities is not a great idea when your body is still getting used to an upside-down time zone.

If you're in the same time zone as your hometown, of course, you can skip this part and dive straight into getting to know your new surrounds.

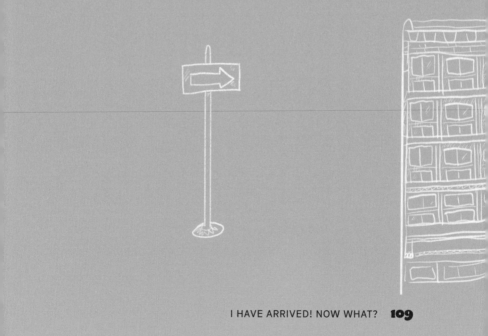

What can I do to stave off jet lag?

Not a great deal, unfortunately, other than trying to go to bed at night and get up in the morning, rather than the other way around, which is what your body will be trying to force you to do. This won't necessarily stave off jet lag, but it can help you adjust to your new time zone a little faster.

As an aside, I've always found prescription melatonin helpful for overcoming jet lag and insomnia, but it's not to everyone's taste. Some people suffer side effects like headaches, nausea, and fatigue (of course, fatigue IS kind of what you're looking for when you take melatonin, but it should not leave you feeling sluggish the next day). Melatonin is a naturally occurring hormone that helps signal to your body that it's time to sleep, and while it's a far gentler option than a conventional sleeping pill, you should still discuss the possible side effects with your doctor before deciding to use it. Always visit your doctor before travel (*see* p.54) and test out any new medication you're planning on taking before you leave, so you know how it will affect you.

Magnesium pills could be another option, but check with your doctor first to make sure it won't interfere with any medications you may be taking. Topically applied lavender oil has few side effects and could be worth trying if you're struggling to sleep but don't want to use medication.

I stink after travel, what should I do?

Instead of lying down, have a wash. This is important to do ASAP because the way you smell after a long journey is going to really lower your opinion of yourself. The human body is both a marvel and a slime-addled vessel of filth. Never have I been more aware of this than when peeling off my clothes after a long-haul flight, and given that I live in Australia, seven billion nautical miles from anywhere else in the world, *every* flight is a long-haul flight. The way I smell after 26 hours in transit can only be described as an open-air food market in Chernobyl circa '86, abruptly abandoned in the wake of the explosion, with all the vegetables, fruit, meat, and fish left to rot in the radioactive sun.

Washing will also reinvigorate you so you are ready to explore. Make sure you put on fresh clothes after your shower, and preferably some nice-smelling moisturiser or hand cream, which will help to re-humanise you after your travels. Think of it as an embalmer would: your job is to make the corpse look and smell presentable.

Walk the earth

After you've washed, get out and go for a short walk around the block. Leave the unpacking for later, when you are devilishly tired but trying to hold out as long as possible before going to bed. Walking helps you get more quickly acquainted with your new surroundings, which in turn dissolves some of your *where-the-hell-am-I?* anxiety. Make a note of anything close by that interests you to revisit later when you are human again.

Go to the local grocery or convenience store and buy a few essentials – bread, chocolate, two-minute noodles – so you've got something on hand should the urge to eat dinner at 3am strike (I have eaten many spanakopitas in the small hours of the morning, held hostage to a jet-lagged body that firmly believes it is 7pm, and therefore time to consume large quantities of hot food).

It may sound a banal way to begin a holiday, but spending half an hour mooching around the grocery store will give you a far better feel for where you are than any crowded tourist attraction ever could. Grocery stores, cafes, markets and parks are where you'll find the locals going about their regular business, and one of the best parts of visiting any new place is simply seeing how other people live.

Hotel room tip

Liesl Ruff is a long-standing hotel room aficionado and frequent flyer, and she says: 'I like to head straight to my hotel room, order room service, watch foreign game shows on TV and decompress. Then I'll go out to the grocery or corner store and buy a cup of noodles, mac and cheese and anything else that can be made with boiling water. I do have a phobia of hotel and motel kettles, as I've heard people use them to wash their underpants, but I'm trying to get over it.'

Make friends with maps

Hotels and hostels can usually provide you with local maps, and it's a good idea to familiarise yourself with them before you head out so you feel less panicked at the prospect of your phone battery dying while you're out and about. It also enables you to look confident while navigating a new place, so you're more likely to look like a seasoned local rather than a vulnerable tourist. Having said that, if you do need to look at a map or ask for directions, find someone in the crowd who doesn't look like a serial killer, and go ahead and ask them for help. It's better than getting lost, which will increase your anxiety levels a lot more than chatting to a stranger.

Seeing the Popular Places

(without raising your blood pressure)

You can't go to Paris without seeing the Louvre, Tour
Eiffel and Notre Dame. Except, of course, you can.
You can do whatever you want. It's your holiday. You'll
find everyone has very strong ideas about what you must
do on your holiday. Don't let other people's expectations
dictate what you choose to see and do.

If all you want to do while you're in Paris is eat croissants until your blood turns to butter and wander the streets marvelling at how much prettier Saint-Germain-des-Prés is than, say, anywhere else in the world, that's fine. It's more than fine; it's what most people would probably do if they just took a deep breath and asked themselves 'What do I actually want to do today?' The Eiffel Tower is beautiful but, ultimately, it's just a very tall iron structure. You've seen it on a thousand postcards. It's not terribly… surprising.

That said, the world's major tourist draws are popular for good reason (mostly), and it is possible to visit them while minimising your exposure to lines and crowds. If you're wanting to visit eternally popular destinations like the Taj Mahal, Vatican or Versailles, consider going in the off-season. In other words, when it's not peak tourist season. Europe, for example, is a shit-fight all summer long because, well, Europe in summer is hard to beat. You are going to have to make peace with crowds if this is when you travel. But you might want to travel in what's called the shoulder seasons, those either side of the peak times, like spring and autumn. This means you'll still get a lot of beautiful weather, but less of the crowds. You'll also have a wider choice of accommodation to book.

When visiting tourist hot spots, do some research before you go to get an idea of when the quieter times are – a good general rule of thumb is very early in the morning or later in the afternoon close to closing time. If you're visiting the Tower of London, for example, avoid doing so in the British school holidays, as it will be overrun with screeching children on school excursions shoving carrot sticks up their nostrils and elbowing you out of view of the Crown Jewels. The Museum of Modern Art in New York draws around six million visitors per year, and is rammed with art-hungry cheapskates on Friday afternoons, when admission is waived, so if you're crowd-phobic don't plan a Friday visit. And the Sydney Opera House doesn't need to be seen at ultra-close range – there are plenty of gorgeous and comparatively quiet spots along the Harbour from which to ogle its pleasing curves.

Taking the road less travelled

You could also investigate travelling to lesser-known destinations. This is a great way to do your bit to prevent over-tourism, a clunky phrase describing a serious problem. While the idea of any place at all being overwhelmed with tourists seems frankly absurd at the time of writing, when the COVID-19 pandemic has all but shuttered the world, over-tourism poses a serious threat. In popular destinations like Phuket, Dubrovnik and Venice, relentless crowds have contributed to damaged ecosystems and badly impacted quality of life for the locals – many of whom have been forced to leave. There are plenty of websites and blogs covering ethical and sustainable travel that can help you find interesting alternatives to oversubscribed destinations.

If you are visiting popular destinations, you can still make a difference by avoiding cruise ships and large group travel, which contribute to over-tourism while not giving much back to the local economy. Instead, only book through local, ethical tour operators. Go to local shops and restaurants, and avoid the big chain hotels and restaurants. There are usually local groups on the ground that promote sustainable eateries, attractions and activities and can help guide you.

Navigating food intolerances

Food intolerances and allergies can cause anxiety when travelling, even if they're not something you have to pay much attention to on home turf. Each new country has its own culture and customs around food, and navigating these with the added baggage of any complex dietary requirements can feel daunting. Unfortunately, food intolerances are not nearly as easy to lose as your passport, but plenty of people with special dietary requirements manage to travel while enjoying the local cuisine – it's simply a matter (again) of doing your research before you go.

Before you arrive, look into which cafes and restaurants offer vegan and gluten-free options, and get an approximate idea of the local cuisine so you know what will and won't be safe to eat for you. Write down the name and location of a couple of health or wholefoods grocery stores and supermarkets (which exist in almost every city these days) – they usually have a broad selection of foods that cater to special dietary requirements.

If you have a food allergy or are on a special diet, you should also make language prep an integral part of your planning. Learn basic phrases like, 'I am allergic to ...'; 'No dairy'; or 'Vegan'. If you still feel shaky about your ability to clearly communicate, there are apps – Equal Eats, Allergy Translate – that can do this on your behalf. It's also wise to think about booking accommodation with kitchen facilities so you can prepare your own food as much as possible. That doesn't mean you'll miss out on sampling the local cuisine – there will be plenty of that on offer in the supermarkets and delis.

If your dietary preferences are not based around allergies or serious intolerances, you may find you have a more flexible attitude towards what you eat while you're away. I rarely eat meat at home, but when I visit Germany I become rabidly carnivorous, my usually non-existent appetite for meat dialled up to 11. This is not for lack of vegetarian options, which are plentiful; I just can't say no to bratwurst, and bratwurst, true to stereotype, is abundant, delicious and cheap in Germany.

Capturing your holiday

There is nothing wrong with documenting your holiday or sharing snaps on social media, as long as you always remember that your holiday is for *you* to enjoy, not your social media followers. Trying to capture the perfect moment to share can become a chore, sucking the joy and spontaneity out of your travels. Obsessively documenting your holiday can make it feel as if you're removed from it, and, frankly, when you've invested a lot of your own money into a trip, you don't want to be experiencing any of it at a distance.

Then there's the murky area where you start comparing your experience to what you're seeing in other people's photos. Most holiday snaps we see on social media have been carefully staged, curated and filtered to project an image of endless fun and frivolity, and rarely reflect the true nature of travel, which is by turns unpredictable, exhilarating, exhausting, disappointing, moving, confusing and grubby. The surest way to ruin your holiday (and your life) is by comparing it to other people's. Try and use your holiday to wind back rather than rev up your social media presence. Remember that if you didn't photograph it, it still happened. I don't have any photos of the time I passed a gallstone, but I remember it very well nonetheless. There are no photos of me as a newborn, yet my mum does not have trouble recalling any of the details of my birth. Your brain takes more photos than your iPhone and files away them neatly in your hippocampus, like fleshy cloud storage.

One of the most unexpected and thrilling parts of travel is the permission you suddenly have to be whoever you want to be. The rest of the world knows nothing about you. There is no need to keep up the performative aspect of who you are at home – the careful person or the studious person or the impulsive, fun person – you are entirely relieved of this burden. What a shame, then, to squander that precious opportunity to find another side of yourself because you're trying to comply with the social media Holiday Commandments (thou shalt be pictured looking sultry and hot in a bikini, thou shalt be pictured looking solemn and hot in front of a historical monument, thou shalt be pictured looking zany and hot while jumping for joy in the waves, etc!)

Decide on some social media boundaries for yourself, and try to stick to them. My holiday photo rule is no selfies. The Spanish Steps, the Taj Mahal, the Pyramids of Giza: these things are interesting enough. They don't need my face next to them to spice them up.

Anxiety ratings of popular attractions

Little to no Anxiety

Medium Anxiety

High Anxiety

Eiffel Tower, Paris, France

Big queues and a wait for the lift
if you want to climb at peak times

Sundown visit, no climb

Disney World, Florida, USA

Weekdays off-season, early in
the day

Weekends peak season

MoMA, New York, USA

Friday afternoon

Early afternoon weekdays

Acropolis, Athens, Greece

Sunset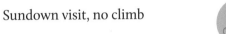

Any other time of day

La Sagrada Familia, Barcelona, Spain

Booked ahead/early in the morning

Not booked ahead/middle of the day

Angkor Wat, Cambodia

5am or 4pm

Midday

Taj Mahal, India

Sunrise

Any other time of day

Bondi Beach, Australia

Weekday mornings, autumn and spring

Weekends, spring and summer

Forbidden City, Beijing, China

Weekdays, after 2pm

Weekends, midday

Colosseum, Italy

Anytime in July and August

Any time other than July and August in the early morning

Tate Modern, London, UK

Sunday morning 10am

Weekdays after 10am

Pyramids, Cairo, Egypt

24/7

Any Popular Tourist Spot

Midweek; midday; peak season; school holidays

Q&A
with
Emily Scott

Registered Nurse and
American Travel Blogger
of *Two Dusty Travelers*

What ignited your passion for travel and, specifically, ethical/sustainable travel?

My parents are avid travelers, so I was brought up traveling. I've always been a bleeding heart and wanted to leave the world better than it was when I entered it – and when I'm traveling, that part of me doesn't shut off (even if sometimes I wish it would!).

Unfortunately, tourism has the power to destroy the world's most beautiful places – if we're not careful. When I see trash on a beach, I want to pick it up; when I watch elephants on safari, I want to help protect them; when I see locals trapped in poverty just steps away from fancy resorts, I want to address that inequity.

I've found that travel is so much more special if I'm able to give back or uplift the place I'm visiting in some way, even if it's small. It often leads me to the most amazing local guides, restaurants, markets and adventures.

You travelled to West Africa as a global health/disaster response nurse during the last major Ebola outbreak. Can you tell me about 'voluntourism'?

I became a nurse because I wanted to have a skill that would allow me to travel anywhere in the world and be useful. It has been a lot of work to gain the necessary experience and learn to avoid the pitfalls of humanitarian work ('voluntourism' is a lucrative industry, and it's easy for foreign volunteers to cause harm, despite good intentions). But the payoff has been worth it, as I'm able to spend several weeks each year on global health assignments or deploying to disasters. At home, I traded my full-time nursing job for a per diem position with fewer benefits and less consistency, but it gives me the freedom to take off on a moment's notice (after the 2015 earthquake in Nepal, I was on a plane to Kathmandu within a few days).

Even when I'm traveling for global health work, there's still time off to explore. I'll never forget spending my day off at a pristine beach in Sierra Leone during the Ebola outbreak, squeezing in a weekend safari while working at a refugee clinic in Northern Uganda or flying through town on a motorcycle tour while volunteering in Haiti. For me, it's the perfect balance and I feel incredibly lucky that I've been able to carve out this niche.

What kind of strategies did you find useful for managing trepidation before going to work in an Ebola hot zone?

I was anxious before leaving to work in Sierra Leone! I remember putting on a happy face while saying goodbye to my family at the airport, and then crying in a bathroom stall after I got through security.

I try to think of everything as a risk-benefit analysis. I knew the risks of working in an Ebola outbreak were serious, but the benefits were pretty incredible: the ability to literally save lives and help stop an epidemic. I decided that I wouldn't be able to live with myself if I let my fear keep me at home when I knew I had the skills that West Africa desperately needed. Once I was on the ground in Sierra Leone, I knew I had done everything I could to prepare and that I had to just trust my skills and protective equipment.

What changes in travel would you like to see after the COVID pandemic?

I would like to see people think more about the effect we have on the places we visit. Post-pandemic travel will definitely involve more research and planning around the risk to ourselves and others. But this applies to much more than viruses. Every decision we make – where we stay, how we get there, where we spend our tourist dollars – has real consequences for local communities. I think COVID has proven how deeply interconnected we all are, and that a problem in a distant place may not remain distant for long. We're all in this together, and we have a responsibility to care for each other.

What are some of the things we can do to make sure we're respecting the people and places we're visiting?

Always treat the place you're visiting the way you would want visitors to treat your hometown! Take a little bit of time to learn about where you're going so you can respect the local culture. Follow the rules and be kind, like you would at home – just because you're on vacation doesn't mean you get to climb over a railing to get that Instagram shot or leave your trash behind.

Also, think critically about where your money is going! Every dollar you spend is like a vote – do you want it to go to massive international hotel and restaurant chains or to local businesses? I do my best to stay at locally owned accommodations, eat at local restaurants and spend my tourist dollars at businesses that support the local community.

What's your best piece of advice for young women planning their first big trip?

Go for it! It's okay to be scared and do it anyway. Most of the big decisions that ended up changing my life for the better scared the hell out of me as I was actually taking the plunge. I have a little quote taped to my bathroom mirror that says, 'If your dreams don't scare you, they're not big enough.'

Also, seek out women's travel groups in the places you're visiting. Even if you're traveling 'solo', that doesn't mean you have to be alone – with social media you can find women travelers to meet up with just about anywhere.

What basic hygiene precautions and first-aid essentials would you recommend for travel?

Wash your hands before you eat, and try to keep your hands off your face.

If you're traveling to a developing country or very rural area, keep in mind that the food and water may have bugs in it that your system isn't used to! My motto is: boil it, cook it, peel it or forget it.

I always travel with a small first-aid kit (in my carry-on). I add or remove things based on the destination, but the staples include Band-Aids, tweezers, small scissors, ziplock bags (to make ice packs), a thermometer, my preferred cold and pain relief medicines, electrolyte tablets to put in water (in case of vomiting/diarrhoea, or even just if I'm going somewhere very hot).

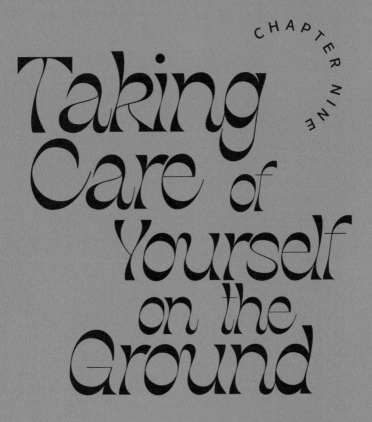

Taking Care of Yourself on the Ground

CHAPTER NINE

You travel o'er land and sea to expand your horizons, open your mind, see the world, learn how to say 'A triple scoop cone, please' in Italian (*'tre balle di gelato, per favore'*), walk the Camino, pocket a pebble at the Berlin Wall, but also to HAV SUM FUN IN THE CLUBS AMIRITE?

Meeting new people, hanging out in bars, finding yourself at a party in an unknown corner of an unknown city – these are traditional rites of passage for many young travellers. If partying is not your bag, don't feel obliged to dive headlong into the nightlife. For every twinge of the fear of missing out (FOMO) one experiences, there is a satisfying sigh of the joy of missing out (JOMO). The older you get, the stronger the JOMO gets. By the time you're 40, the thing you enjoy most about travel will probably be food. The thing you enjoy most about *life* will probably be food.

But making new friends, finding new travel companions and dancing with strangers in bars can be a lot of fun. You just need to stick to the same personal safety rules you would follow at home, with minor tweaks to account for the fact that you are a tourist, and therefore – in the nicest possible way – a bit dumb.

Being a bit dumb is not without its benefits. One of the things I enjoy most about being in a country where I cannot speak the language is not understanding what the hell people are talking about. When I am privy to strangers' conversations in English, at least half of what I hear makes me mutter 'FFS' under my breath. Erroneously, I assume that dumb conversations happen only in English and that French people on the Metro speak only of Foucault and Descartes. Which is dumb.

But not speaking the language can also make you vulnerable, as you have no idea if the person seated next to you at the bar is talking to their friend about post-structuralism or how to bury the body of a foreign tourist so it will never be found. It's a good idea to learn a few basic phrases, such as: 'Hello, how are you?', 'Can you please point me in the direction of …?', 'Where is the hospital?', and 'Are you an axe-murderer?'. You should do this as both a courtesy to the locals (as there is nothing more uncouth than an English-speaking tourist who assumes they will be understood by everyone, everywhere) and as a safety precaution for yourself.

Talk like a local – aka language apps

I always immerse myself (learn at least three words) in the local lingo before I travel to a new country. My favourite language app is Duolingo because it's important to me that I'm able to say, 'My uncle has a horse', 'The bride is a squirrel' and 'This cheese is good, though it is old' wherever I go. Download a bunch of free language apps to start with, and work out which best suits you. Mondly, Memrise, Busuu and Babbel all have plenty of fans.

No matter how diligently you practice, it's impossible to learn an entire language in a few weeks (unless you're a hyper-polyglot), so alongside your language learning app, you'll need a good translating app. I always use Google Translate, as I find it gives the least 'drunk relative at Christmas lunch' sounding translations. When I had to spend four days in hospital in Sicily with my daughter, none of the doctors spoke English. I relied almost entirely on Google Translate to communicate, occasionally calling for backup via phone from my dad, a fluent speaker of Italian, who spent more time discussing Formula One season with the doctors than his granddaughter's medical care, which just goes to show you that sometimes it really is safer to rely on machines than humans. Ideally, you would be using Google Translate to

read street signs and menus rather than have conversations about IV drips and blood sugar levels, but in a pinch, it will do the trick.

Don't forget the value of bodily gestures; they are almost universally understood, although it pays to do your research before you leave so that you're across any cultural differences: in the Balkans, for instance, nodding means 'no' and shaking your head means 'yes'.

Look like a local, act like a local

One of the most universally accepted rules of travel safety is that you should always do your best to blend in with the locals. Do not have Google Maps open and giving audible directions. Keep Google Translate at a discreet volume. For the love of God, don't hang a camera around your neck or kit yourself out in glaringly obvious tourist garb. As much as is feasible, try to dress like a local. In Melbourne, where I live, this simply means wearing either a) a lot of black, b) a lot of 'Fun Mum' prints or c) a lot of athleisure wear. No one in Australia *ever* wears Akubra hats, unless they own a sheep station or are Molly Meldrum (our premier pop star interviewer of the '80s and '90s). Parisians do not wear berets, despite what *Emily in Paris* would have us believe, and Italians are not all Armani-clad supermodels.*

Being aware of how the locals dress will help you to avoid making a sore-thumb fashion mistake, like wearing a black lace mantilla to buy churros in Barcelona. Be mindful of cultural norms and the fact that in certain places, you will need to dress modestly and/or cover up, both out of respect to the locals and as a safety precaution. In temples and mosques, for example, your shoulders and knees should be covered – and often your hair. In Italy, you must cover your shoulders when visiting the Vatican, and you'll find most places of worship have similar dress codes. In many countries, showing a lot of skin is frowned upon, just like wearing flip-flops to upmarket restaurants is. In North Korea and Sudan, women are not allowed to wear trousers.

* except in Milan, where they actually are, even the ones who work at the airport Europcar.

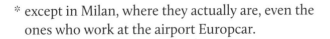

Don't tell everyone you're a tourist

Don't advertise your foreigner status when you're out and about. I once ate a pizza that wound up costing *one hundred and seventy dollars,* on account of me being very clearly not Italian, and therefore eligible for the dramatically inflated tourist rate. The pizza was good, but at *one and hundred and seventy dollars*, you want it do something more than just ... be a pizza. Give you a lap dance, for instance, or do your taxes.

If a cab driver or Uber driver asks you if it's the first time you've been here, tell them 'no', as your first-timer status can see you being taken for a ride – literally via lengthy, traffic-laden routes and exorbitant fares. Always take a photo of your cab driver's number plate and ID, and make sure the meter is running at all times. Check this before you get in, as tourists are frequently informed the meter is broken. In some countries you can agree on a price to get from point A or B to start with, but note they might charge you extra if you stop at some sights along the way.

Some people just plain hate tourists, for reasons both fair and unfair, and this is another compelling reason to keep your foreigner status as discreet as possible. As someone who lives in a tourist hot spot, I can attest to the fact that the sight of a sunburnt Brit necking a beer in a Bintang tank top does nothing to enhance my mood. Many places must walk the fine line between encouraging tourism for the health of their local economy, while simultaneously trying to prevent it from being swallowed alive by visitors. Even if you feel you're being harangued on every corner by operators keen to squeeze a buck out of you, try to treat them with patience and respect. I have witnessed many a rude tourist on beaches overseas telling the sunglass or pineapple hawkers to piss off, and it makes my blood boil. This is likely their only source of income and you are enjoying yourself in their hometown.

Seize the day(time)

We've talked about the benefits to your body clock of immediately adopting the local time for sleeping and waking, but there's also a safety benefit; it's safer to be out and about during the day pretty much everywhere in the world. This is not a finger-wagging order to keep yourself secured in a turret, knitting blankets for injured animals every night. If the nightlife is your thing, you have every right to get out there and make the most of it. Unfortunately, a simple, if tiresome, reality is that there are going to be people you don't want to cross paths with in every city you visit, and there are more of them around at night. This is advice both women *and* men should heed.

Daylight is your friend in a foreign city. You'll see much more of the place by limiting the number of night-time bacchanals you partake in. My personal view on this is that full-tilt holiday hedonism is a waste of time. Drunken nights on the dance floor might be what you need to get you through the

banal grind of daily life *at home* – to momentarily escape the reality of your overdue uni assignment, your crap boss, your mother's hip replacement operation, your cats inflammatory bowel disease and trichomoniosis diagnosis (or maybe that's just me). When you're on holiday, you're *on holiday* – day-to-day life should not be stressful. There is no need to escape day-to-day *holiday* life. Again, if the nightlife is your thing, go for it, but try not to let it eat up too many of your precious daylight hours, which is the only time you can actually, literally, *see* stuff.

Always have an escape plan

At the beginning of every flight, the cabin crew will show you where your nearest exits are and ask you to commit them to memory. The same principle should apply wherever you go: always have an escape plan. For every theatre, museum, gallery, cafe, bar, tourist attraction, metro, nightclub and supermarket you walk into, know how to walk out just as easily. Planning in advance how you'll manage in an emergency or where there may be a threat to your safety can actually *help* you feel less anxious. Instead of thinking, 'What if terrorists storm the Louvre?!', try thinking, 'What will I *do* if terrorists storm the Louvre?'

Identify your fears, think about your worst-case scenario and plan for it. This doesn't mean you need to spend hours and hours perfecting watertight emergency protocols – it simply means you need to know where the exits are and where you would turn for help if you needed it. And remember that people will always help you – whether in an emergency or giving you directions. Survivors of the 9/11 attack reported that evacuees in the tower stairwells showed an uncommon level of patience and understanding towards one another. Humans tend to treat each other better in a crisis.

There are some universal basic safety guidelines you should always adhere to: always knowing where you are going in advance, sharing your itinerary with at least one friend or family member, trusting your instincts (*see* p.17) and always carrying some local currency (*see* p.78).

Socialising for the socially anxious

I am the person least likely, at face value, to be labelled socially anxious. I find it easy to talk to people, I always have something to say and I don't have many conversational boundaries.

And yet I would almost always rather be at home than at any kind of social event, no matter how much I like the company. I look at going to parties as a chore, like vacuuming, except that vacuuming doesn't ask anything of me other than that I, literally, suck; I wish the rest of the world expected as little of me as my vacuum cleaner does. I value social interactions, but I prefer them to be quick and spontaneous. It's said that the ideal length of a sexual encounter is between seven and 13 minutes and, for me, the same formula applies to socialising.

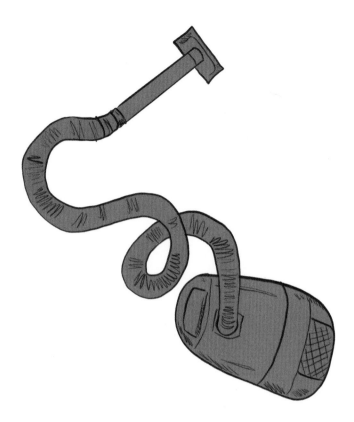

Everyone experiences a pang of social anxiety from time to time, but it pays to try and push through this when you're travelling, as there are so many opportunities to further expand your holiday horizons when you open yourself up to meeting new people. Hanging out in the lobby of popular hostels is an easy way to make new acquaintances. Every new connection you make helps to chip away a little of your social anxiety and bolster your confidence. My social anxiety, along with almost all of my anxiety, is largely anticipatory. I don't actually find it hard to talk to people; I find it hard to *think* about talking to people.

But I am too shy to hang out in a hostel lobby!

So, try doing this instead:

- Reach out via your social networks to see if you know anyone who lives in the places you're visiting, or knows someone else who lives there. Ask if they'd be open to meeting up for a coffee or showing you around. This is an easy way to make an immediate social connection wherever you go, and most of us now have large and diverse enough social media connections to ensure that you'll know someone with a connection to the place you're going.

- Don't get too hung up on always pushing beyond your comfort zones. Your holiday doesn't need to be an unending series of personal challenges. Set yourself small goals and see how you go. We are confronted every day of our lives with difficult stuff that we can't do that much about – climate change, pandemics, corporate malfeasance, mac' n' cheese candy canes. Under these circumstances, getting out of bed every day and smiling occasionally is an accomplishment itself. You are travelling – that is plenty brave in itself.

- Book a group tour. You'll get the benefit of a local tour guide and all their insider knowledge, plus you'll meet loads of other travellers with good advice about where to go and what to do, as well what to avoid.

- There are also plenty of apps to help you meet fellow travellers, including some, like Hey! Vina, which are only available to women. Bumble BFF, Tripr, and Patook are all worth having a look at, and all are for platonic hook-ups only.

Reflections on Travel

CHAPTER TEN

The last two years during COVID have occupied the
strange space between panic and boredom; high-level
anxiety colliding with situational apathy. Many of us have
spent this time reflecting on our former lives in the
BC (Before COVID) world, which, as damaged and chaotic
as it was, offered a degree of freedom – physical and
psychological – which we did not quite appreciate
until it was abruptly pulled from under us. Pandemics
aren't a unique feature of human existence;
they're just new to all of us who weren't around for
the Spanish Flu in 1918, which is … all of us.

During 2020, when my hometown was locked down and reassurance and comfort were in short supply, I found a sweet spot to visit inside my head: my memories of travelling. Travel takes you out of the everyday and into the unknown, where you discover things about people and places and yourself that cannot be accessed any other way. It's so easy to feel like your world is small and restrictive but travel reminds you that it's not, and memories of travel take you away from the daily routine.

Sometimes I would think about landing in Bologna in 2014, ready for the mortuary slab after 48 hours in transit, but miraculously revived as I emerged from the airport and realised it was *Summer in Italy,* I was in a beautiful ancient city and there was pizza on every-second street corner. The small, budget-yet-Baroque hotel we stayed in dished up the best breakfast of my life – the best croissants, the best fruit, the best hot chocolate. There was nothing luxe or unique about any of it; it was good, simple food prepared with care, and it was my first morning in Bologna. Sometimes that's all that's required to make a permanent impression.

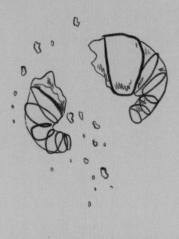

Other times I would take myself back to North Queensland, where I spent a few months in 2011, to a special part of the Noosa National Park where the forest meets the Pacific Ocean. I would pause for a few minutes at a small lookout point on my daily walk, sucking in great lungfuls of ocean air while I watched the sun light up the waves. It was a hard time in my life; I was a young single mother and lonely as hell. When I stood there at the lookout, just for a few minutes, I felt everything would be okay. I was not used to feeling that way. I could gain some respite from 2020 and its awfulness by closing my eyes and putting myself back in this time, in a place where everything felt hopeful and pure and good.

Often, I would think about my first cab ride from Tegel Airport into Berlin and how palpably I could feel the extraordinary, traumatic history of the city coming off the walls and out of the pavement as we made our way into Kreuzberg. All of my family were directly impacted by World War II, and to be at the epicentre of its origins was an overwhelming experience. Later, after the ecstatic discovery that our apartment on Kottbusser Damm was not a dive (as was often the case in the early days of Airbnb), I went downstairs to buy lunch and discovered the world's best Turkish take-out right opposite our apartment block. I've made this cafe the cornerstone of every travel decision I've made since, which, admittedly, has somewhat limited my travel options.

Where in my head would I have sought refuge if I didn't have these experiences? To my memories of verifying my identity when picking up packages at the post office? Of cleaning the kitty litter tray after switching from wet food to kibble (wild a ride as that was)? Of catching the tram to work and trying not to audibly fart (also kind of a wild ride, admittedly)? Savouring the small pleasures of day-to-day life is vitally important – it's these small things that get you through life, but you do need to shake it up occasionally with a bit of the extraordinary.

One of the less talked-about benefits of travel is the way it can help you make sense of yourself when your family's origins are elsewhere. It is never less than revelatory to visit the places where your family began. Being the child of a Hungarian migrant and the granddaughter of a Russian/French migrant, I have never felt particularly *of* my own country: I was born in Australia and have never lived anywhere else, but growing up, I was acutely aware, despite my fair skin and blue eyes, that I was not like the other Aussie kids. My dad did not dress, speak or behave like other Australian dads; he was a fabric wholesaler who preferred shopping for clothes and smoking cigars to footy and beer.

My favourite thing to do as a child was to simply sit outside the door to my dad's office, listening to him speak German, French, Italian and Hungarian to his friends, clients and family across the globe. The soothing tones and inflections of all those indecipherable languages worked brilliantly as a pre-bedtime balm for my worried young head. Every night, people from all over the world temporarily occupied a room in our home, as my dad discussed the price of jersey with Franco in Milan or the new season's silks with Helmut in Cologne. Travelling brings me that exact same feeling of wonder and connection every single time – be it domestically or internationally, it is always *elsewhere*, and elsewhere is endlessly exciting.

It is a special privilege to see how other people live, to realise that every culture – even within your own country – has added their own flourishes and traditions to the day-to-day business of living, making it up as they go along and, usually, miraculously, making it work. I did not really make sense to myself until I went to the places where my father and grandfather were born and raised. The sense of relief I felt at discovering there was a whole continent where I didn't feel like an outsider looking in (though I sounded, if not looked, like an alien to everyone else) had the curious effect of making me feel more connected to my actual country of birth. From a distance, in a place where I felt very much at home, I was finally able to identify the ways in which I was, actually, uniquely Australian.

So do it. Travel. Don't do it because of any neat ideas about conquering your anxiety. In all likelihood, you will not 'conquer' your anxiety; most chronic illnesses cannot be 'conquered'. But you can learn to manage it, live with it, and you can – I PROMISE – travel and survive and spend the rest of your life, whatever else happens in it, extremely happy that you went out on a limb and dove into the unknown. You'll have a bank of memories and experiences to draw from at any time, and as we all now know a little too well, memories can be everything in hard times.

Just steer clear of the capsicum dip.

References

Australia

- https://www.headtohealth.gov.au/
- https://www.sane.org/
- https://beyondblue.org.au

United Kingdom

- https://www.mind.org.uk/
- https://www.mentalhealth.org.uk/

United States:

- https://www.nimh.nih.gov/
- https://www.cdc.gov/mentalhealth/tools-resources/individuals/index.htm

Citations

PAGE 11 (illustration) – Yayoi Kusama

PAGE 16 – Power, Robert A & Steinberg, Stacy + 27 authors, 8 June 2015, 'Polygenic risk scores for schizophrenia and bipolar disorder predict creativity', Nature Neuroscience.

PAGE 28 – 'Growing UP with Anxiety: Lena Dunham and Dr Marie Albano in Conversation with Jenni Konner', YouTube, uploaded Feb 8 2017.

PAGE 83 – NTSB Safety Report March 2001, 'Survivability of Accidents Involving Part 121 U.S Air Carrier Operations 1983 Through 2000'.

About the author

Bunny Banyai is an author, freelance journalist and copywriter based in Melbourne, Australia. She has spent most of her life anticipating the worst and hoping for the best. She loves cats, roller-skating, cats, reading about infectious diseases – and cats.

Acknowledgments

Many thanks to the fantastic team at Hardie Grant for their patience and support: publisher Melissa Kayser, project editor Megan Cuthbert, illustrator and designer Astred Hicks, proofreader Lyric Dodson, and editor Alice Barker, whose endless reassurance and cheerleading got me through to the finish line.

Many thanks also to Emily Scott, Maggie Mazur, Libby Bakewell and Casey Donovan for their contributions, Liesl Ruff, Larissa Dubecki, and Rose Bessette for their travel tips, Maggie Vandeleur for her friendship, Kirsten W. for the therapy, and Tom Carlyon for his love and great hair.

Published in 2021 by Hardie Grant Explore, an imprint of Hardie Grant Publishing

Hardie Grant Explore (Melbourne)
Wurundjeri Country
Building 1, 658 Church Street
Richmond, Victoria 3121

Hardie Grant Explore (Sydney)
Gadigal Country
Level 7, 45 Jones Street
Ultimo, NSW 2007

www.hardiegrant.com/au/explore

A catalogue record for this
book is available from the
National Library of Australia

Hardie Grant acknowledges the Traditional Owners of the Country on which
we work, the Wurundjeri people of the Kulin Nation and the Gadigal people
of the Eora Nation, and recognises their continuing connection to the land,
waters and culture. We pay our respects to their Elders past and present.

Anxious Girls Do It Better
ISBN 9781741177275

10 9 8 7 6 5 4 3 2 1

Publisher: Melissa Kayser
Project editor: Megan Cuthbert
Editor: Alice Barker
Proofreader: Lyric Dodson
Design and illustrations: Astred Hicks
Typesetting: Susanne Geppert

Colour reproduction by Susanne Geppert and Splitting Image Colour Studio

Printed and bound in China by LEO Paper Products LTD.